Nelson Speaks

NELSON SPEAKS

ADMIRAL LORD NELSON IN HIS OWN WORDS

Joseph F. Callo

Naval Institute Press
Annapolis, Maryland

Naval Institute Press
291 Wood Road
Annapolis, MD 21402

Library of Congress Cataloging-in-Publication Data
    Callo, Joseph F., 1929–
        Nelson speaks: Admiral Lord Nelson in his own words
    / Joseph F. Callo.
            p. cm.
        Includes bibliographical references (p.) and index.
        ISBN 1-55750-199-8 (acid-free paper)
            1. Great Britain—History, Naval—Quotations, max-
    ims, etc. 2. Admirals—Great Britain—Biography—
    Sources. 3. Naval art and science—Quotations, maxims,
    etc. 4. Naval history—Quotations, maxims, etc. I. Nelson,
    Horatio Nelson, Viscount, 1758–1805 Quotations. II. Title.

    DA87.1N4 C26 2001

                                            00-050020

Printed in the United States of America on acid-free paper ∞
07 06 05 04 03 02 01 00   9 8 7 6 5 4 3 2
First printing

All illustrations are from the author's collection.

*Frontispiece: Lieutenant Nelson Volunteering to Board a Prize in
a Violent Gale, November 20, 1777;* engraving by A. Raimbach,
from a painting by Richard Westall

To my grandchildren, Emily, Tomas, Jacob, Audra,
Rima, David, Henry, Jordan, Benedict, Kelsey, and Zoe.
And to those sailors of the U.S. Navy, from admirals
to seamen, who showed me the importance of leading by
example.

Contents

Foreword

"It is the custom, and a very bad one, for the English never to tell their own story." So wrote Admiral Horatio Nelson to Sir Alexander Ball on 7 November 1803 while off the Madalena Islands. Perhaps his observation is true, but Nelson may not have thought it such a bad custom to let others tell his story had he been able to read Captain Alfred Thayer Mahan's *The Life of Nelson* at the other end of the nineteenth century. Mahan's American work is arguably the finest and most comprehensive Nelson biography ever written, so perhaps people do see themselves more clearly through the eyes of others.

The author of this book, Joe Callo, is also an American with a United States Navy background. Callo follows in Mahan's wake not by producing yet another among the many Nelson biographies but rather by seeking to understand the subject better. In so doing, Callo delves beneath the carefully constructed public image of Nelson the Hero to get at Nelson the Man. Why has Nelson fascinated so many people over so many generations? What was it about his charismatic personality and art of leadership that made both officers and men—often pressed men—eagerly follow him straight into the cannon smoke? It is easier to bring into focus the life of one of Nelson's captains, about whom perhaps only a little has been recorded, than it is to see Nelson, a man about whom hundreds of books have been written over a two-hundred-year span, with any degree of clarity. We stand too close to the flame; the more we look the less we see. Our vision of Nelson has become blurred and our senses dulled by a myriad of preconceived, hero-worshipping, over-familiar images. Much of this has derived from the calculated public relations expertise of the old Navy League during the Victorian era, who had their own urgent agenda and had to promote the Royal Navy in the public mind to increase naval expenditures. What better or more potent instrument than Nelson, who must have seemed heaven-sent for the purpose?

From our own point in time, perhaps the best method of understanding Nelson is to study his letters. Nelson's outpouring, both public and private, was staggering even by the standards of his own day. Joe Callo provides an invaluable introductory guide that will whet the appetite and leave the reader craving more.

The ability to satisfy that craving is easily achieved. We are fortunate in that so many of Nelson's letters not only have survived but have actually been published. Between 1844 and 1846, for example, Sir Nicholas Harris Nicolas edited and annotated seven scholarly volumes of Nelson's *Dispatches and Letters,* and these remain a primary source of Nelson's writings. This work was the pinnacle of a literary career that spanned some twenty-five years and produced an amazing number of books, papers, and articles. It was a career he was forced to seek when in 1816 his first choice, a naval life, came to an abrupt end with the Royal Navy slimming down following Napoleon's defeat. It is chiefly from the deep well of what came to be called "The Nicolas" that Callo draws his inspirational waters for the selection of Nelson's own words.

The story of Nelson's letters, and of how Nicolas came to be involved with them, can be described as picaresque. Nicholas Harris Nicolas was born in Dartmouth, Devon, on 10 March 1799 when England's Revolutionary War with France had already been underway for six years—the length of World War II—and Nelson was already the Hero of the Nile. Nicolas was six-and-a-half-years old when Nelson received his mortal wound at Trafalgar in 1805. Three years later at the age of nine, he followed an elder brother into the Royal Navy as a first-class volunteer. He served under Sir John Duckworth and Lord Exmouth, and he was promoted to lieutenant in September of 1815. He married in 1822 and, discovering that his bride claimed descent from a secretary of state in the reign of Queen Elizabeth, was inspired to investigate her ancestry. Thus, quite by accident, he found himself a new career.

Financial difficulties and the demands of a large family were to eventually drive Nicolas into exile in France. Although England had showered him with honors and literary distinctions for his work on Nelson's letters, pecuniary advantages were meager. He was still scribbling frantically a week before "congestion of the brain" carried him off. Laid to rest in Boulogne cemetery, Nicolas left behind a grieving widow and eight children.

The Nicolas is not the only published source of Nelson's letters, however. In 1809 the Reverend James Stanier Clarke, Chaplain to the Prince of Wales, and John M'Arthur produced the "official" biography of Nelson in two weighty volumes. They had access to Nelson's closest friends and family, all of whom possessed valuable letters. These included Emma Lady Hamilton, Captain Hardy, Earl Nelson, Dr. Beatty, George Rose, and many others. And so it was with great fanfare and the promise of something really special that their work was laid before the public. What they had done was not immediately apparent. While not without merit, and certainly enhanced by Nicholas Pocock's beautiful engravings, Messrs. Clarke and M'Arthur made one terrible mistake: they attempted to "improve" Nelson's letters, with the result that Nelson's own distinctive style was destroyed and his narrative flow lost. In some instances they omitted whole paragraphs and, in others, went so far as to falsify passages to protect reputations. Nicolas himself came face to face with these problems in the 1840s and, where he was unable to consult the original, was forced to copy Clarke and M'Arthur's version. This was made the more tiresome by the fact that the two biographers' widows, still in receipt of letters never returned to their rightful owners, refused Nicolas access. Nevertheless, he made the best of a bad situation.

In 1814, five years after the publication of Clarke and M'Arthur's biography, Thomas Lovewell & Company published two anonymous volumes entitled *The Letters of Lord Nelson to Lady Hamilton; with a Supplement of Interesting Letters, by Distinguished Characters.* This work caused a huge scandal and did a great deal of harm to Nelson's reputation. The first volume contained thirty-nine letters from Nelson to Lady Hamilton plus a supplement with a further thirty-two letters from Nelson's father, his brother William, Earl St. Vincent, Sir Alexander Ball, and others. The second volume contained sixty letters from Nelson to Emma plus a supplement of forty-eight letters from Alexander Davison, Sir William and Lady Hamilton, and others. Nelson had written candidly to Emma under the illusion that she would destroy his letters as he instructed. They not only contained his most private thoughts and opinions, but they also severely criticized some prominent figures in English society; nothing was held back.

By the time of their publication Emma had fled to Calais to escape debtors, and she was immediately accused of having had the letters published, a charge she hotly denied. The letters had, in fact, been stolen from her some years earlier, not by James Harrison, her chosen biographer whom many have blamed, but more likely by a servant called Oliver, a slippery character who bore a bitter grudge against his former employer. Whoever was responsible for the publication of these letters did the evil the perpetrator or perpetrators intended: Emma was pushed toward an early grave and Nelson's reputation was damaged for decades. Some cried forgery, but enough letters have survived for modern research to prove these controversial manuscripts genuine.

Lovewell himself went bankrupt in 1817, and the original letters went to auction. John Wilson Croker, Secretary to the Admiralty, was the successful bidder. When Nicolas was searching for papers nearly thirty years later he was invited to inspect them, although he decided, with a few exceptions, not to publish them. He probably feared the outcry of a new generation. Besides, he had befriended Nelson's daughter, Horatia, and was helping her unravel the mystery of her parentage. Horatia accepted that Nelson was her father but refused to believe the "Lady Hamilton theory" of her birth. The letters leave little doubt as to her mother's identity. Nicolas, who had seen the originals and was in a position to verify their authenticity, must have known the truth but chose to keep silent.

After Croker's death in 1857, the letters found their way into the collection of a Cheshire antiquary, Joseph Mayer. When Mayer died in 1886, the letters (although some had by now gone astray) again went to auction, and this time the purchaser was Sir Thomas Phillips of Middle Hill. After World War II, the collection was acquired by the National Maritime Museum in London.

Another manuscript collector around the time of Mayer and Phillips was Alfred Morrison, and it was he who formed a valuable collection of Nelson-Hamilton letters purchased from various salesrooms during the 1880s. One letter in particular puts beyond any further doubt the true nature of Horatio Nelson and Lady Hamilton's relationship and thereby the parentage of Horatia, although at least one historian and biographer, Hilda Gamlin, was still fighting the platonic corner up to her death in 1899. Morrison, a man of considerable wealth, followed his usual practice with manuscripts he collected by having them printed in two quarto-sized volumes for private circulation. These he distributed among his circle of friends, many of whom, judging by the fact that most copies turn up today unopened, must have dreaded yet another parcel from their rather eccentric benefactor. To those seeking letters from Nelson and the Hamiltons, however, this is indeed a rich vein of veritable gold. They amplify The Nicolas and are recognized as a primary source, made the more valuable by the fact that the whole of Morrison's huge collection was dispersed in a sale at Sotheby's in May 1919, an amazing auction that lasted eighteen days and amounted to 3,300 lots.

Never-before-published Nelson letters continue to turn up in salesrooms and are still being discovered as public collections are electronically cataloged. As a result, it is becoming clear that the great printed sources on which we have relied for so long are incomplete and sometimes—as with Clarke and M'Arthur—inaccurate. For this reason, Colin White of the Royal Naval Museum in Portsmouth is currently assembling material for a new edition of Nelson's collected correspondence, expanding Nicolas's great work to include all the material published or discovered since then.

After Morrison, we have two further important collections of Nelson papers, both published during the 1950s. The first, *Nelson's Letters from the Leeward Islands,* was edited by Geoffrey Rawson and published in a limited edition in 1953 by Golden Cockerel Press. These papers not only shed new light on Nelson's days in the West Indies during the 1780s but publish for the first time the twenty-five letters of the Shirley-Nelson correspondence. The second, *Nelson's Letters to His Wife and Other Documents, 1785–1831,* was edited by George Naish and published in 1958 by Routledge and Keegan Paul in conjunction with the Navy Records Society. This book contains 246 surviving letters from Nelson to Fanny, his wife, published here in full for the first time. Frances Nelson treasured these letters, all that she had left of a husband who had deserted her for Lady Hamilton. After Fanny's death in 1831, the letters were kept in the family until purchased around the turn of the last century by Lady Llangattock, whose collection forms the mainstay of the Nelson Museum at Monmouth. Clarke and M'Arthur had published extracts equal to only about one-third of this collection in 1809, so in the main they were hitherto unpublished.

In the course of these thirteen chapters, Joe Callo takes the reader on a voyage of discovery in which Nelson's character gradually emerges and comes into focus. Nelson was a prolific letter writer and, although like all naval commanders of the period he employed the services of secretaries, a remarkable number of his letters, both professional and private, are written in his own hand. Even after the loss of his right arm, when learning to write with his left hand must have been very difficult, Nelson still preferred to pen his own lines. Although his education before going to sea at age twelve was patchy, he had a good grasp of the English language, was fond of quoting Shakespeare, and had developed the art of letter writing, a trait which perhaps he inherited to some degree from his father but without the Reverend Edmund Nelson's whimsical, early-eighteenth-century style. When Nelson was aware of the public gaze his stance could be almost Churchillian, especially when sniping at the enemy. It might have been Churchill speaking about Hitler when Nelson wrote in 1804: "Buonaparte, by whatever name he may choose to call himself— general, consul, or emperor—is the same man we have always known, and the common disturber of the human race: it is much more dangerous to be his friend than his enemy." Truly it is through his own words that we derive a better understanding of Nelson the Hero and arrive at the core of Nelson the Man.

Michael Nash

Preface

In his 1968 book *Nelson and His World,* noted author Tom Pocock called him "Superman with Everyman's weaknesses." During the two centuries since his death, thousands of books, articles, and dramas have been written about him. The object of Pocock's provocative label and the two-hundred-year stream of literary exploration is Vice Admiral Lord Nelson, a man who shaped history from the decks of his ships.

As the victor at the bloody battles of the Nile, Copenhagen, and Trafalgar, Nelson was one of the world's most successful naval leaders, and in 1897 noted sea power strategist and then–U.S. Navy Captain Alfred Thayer Mahan described him in larger-than-life terms. In *The Life of Nelson,* Mahan called him "the one man who in himself summed up and embodied the greatness of the possibilities which Sea Power comprehends— the man for whom genius and opportunity worked together, to make him the personification of the Navy of Great Britain." In addition, Nelson's brilliant mind and susceptible heart have for two centuries of peace and war generated interest in his life beyond its geopolitical influence. He was a person with great strengths and notable weaknesses, and often it was difficult to separate the two. Those stark contrasts and the depth of his personality are big contributors to his fascination.

Those drawn to highly dramatic personal stories regularly revisit the events of Nelson's life. And that interest has given rise to an entire genre of fiction, epitomized by C. S. Forester's Hornblower series of novels and the more recent Aubrey-Maturin series of sea adventures by Patrick O'Brian. In this book, however, Nelson brings his own unique and highly personal perspective to the circumstances that inspired those immensely popular literary works.

Nelson's enduring significance is underscored by the fact that interest in his life transcends geographical limits, extending far beyond the United Kingdom and even beyond the shores of English-speaking nations. Significant Nelson memorabilia and artifacts can be found not only in places like the Royal Naval Museum in Portsmouth, England, and the Australian National Maritime Museum in Sydney, but also in such diverse countries as Portugal and Japan. They are even found in the museums of countries that were his enemies in combat, such as the Museo Militar in Santa Cruz, Tenerife.

The unique attention to Nelson over the past two centuries raises the question of what it was in his character that made him such a successful naval leader and such a dramatically interesting person. And that question has not fully been answered in the innumerable recountings of the events of his life. This book gives Nelson himself an opportunity to provide revealing answers to that question, a chance to get beyond what he did as a naval officer to what he was as a person. It also provides a resource that can, with study, reveal wisdom that is surprisingly relevant to our own times.

In the following pages, Nelson speaks for himself, mostly through his own writings but, in addition, through reliably attributed statements. The reader can form an opinion of the man almost as if he or she knew him personally. And in that process of allowing Nelson to paint his own portrait his amazing achievements take on new and highly instructive dimensions.

Great Britain has declared the ten years leading up to the bicentennial of the Battle of Trafalgar in 2005 as "The Nelson Decade," creating a special opportunity to view one of history's major players in new ways. It is, coincidentally, an appropriate time in America for a more thorough study of Nelson. For Nelson is not only a military hero of unparalleled dimensions for the British; he had a significant influence on events leading to the radical transformation of the U.S. Navy that took place at the juncture of the nineteenth and twentieth centuries. He was, to a significant extent, an early catalyst of the conversion of the U.S. Navy from the coastal-oriented force of the Civil War into a far-ranging instrument of American global expansion in the late nineteenth century. One of the clearest evidences of this was his obvious influence on Mahan.

Nelson was the quintessential naval combat leader in what was during his time the world's premier navy. As the current occupants of that position of naval leadership, Americans can learn much from Nelson, particularly why he succeeded so spectacularly at times of great danger to his country.

One factor that makes this special view of one of history's leading characters possible is that Nelson was a prolific and talented writer, and much of that writing survived. He could be blunt or flattering, harsh or lyrical, egotistical or humorously self-deprecating. And although there were times when what he wrote was intended for the public domain, most of his writings were extremely frank and private communications. He was not reluctant to expose his feelings on paper, and that openness provides us with a special view of the many dimensions of this unique naval hero's character. A vast amount of those writings were preserved, albeit at times in somewhat adulterated form, in Sir Nicholas Harris Nicolas's seven-volume work, *The Dispatches and Letters of Vice Admiral Viscount Lord Nelson.* Those dispatches and letters and their extensive accompanying footnotes are, with few exceptions, the source for this collection of Nelson's own words. Those interested in unedited letters to Nelson's wife, Fanny, should see George P. B. Naish's *Nelson's Letters to His Wife and Other Documents, 1785–1831.* Those interested in "less edited" letters to Emma Lady Hamilton should see *Memoirs of the Life of Vice-Admiral Lord Viscount Nelson* by Thomas Joseph Pettigrew.

For readers who wish to find the quote in what has come to be known as The Nicolas, or in other references, the source, month, and year of each quotation are provided. Although some of the grammar may seem quaint to the modern reader, Nelson's grammatical constructions and spelling have not been modernized in these selections. In a very few instances, because a quote has particularly broad implications, it is included in more than one chapter.

Accompanying Nelson's own words in this book are illustrations contemporaneous, or nearly contemporaneous, with his life. The artists who created these images, usually in oil or water colors, were among the reporters of Nelson's time. Painters such as Nicholas Pocock, Lemuel Abbott, and Thomas Beechey recorded the major military events and other significant scenes that related to Nelson. And these interpretive "snapshots" are now an integral part of the Nelson persona that has traveled through time.

Of equal importance from the point of view of reportage were the engravers. Highly skilled individuals, such as W. Barnard and J. Fittler, translated original paintings to printing plates by hand, with amazing accuracy. The engravings made it possible for the original images to be reproduced in newspapers, books, and individual engravings. These became the media of the time that accelerated public awareness of Nelson's incredible feats and his establishment as a popular hero of unique proportions. The reader will note that the illustrations accompany particular quotes and are not necessarily in chronological order.

Nelson Speaks begins with a chronological reference for his life. In the chapters that follow that overview, observations and in some cases opinions about his words are provided to put the statements into some context. However, it is left ultimately to the reader to draw his or her own conclusions about the character of Nelson as it is revealed by his own words. And it is hoped that that process will not only enlarge the knowledge of Nelson but will also inspire additional inquiry about why he has earned so much attention for two centuries.

An intriguing clue to the potential for discovery in Nelson's own words was contained in a letter to a friend in 1786. Nelson wrote, "[W]hat I have said is the inward monitor of my heart. . . ." And it is our view of that "inward monitor of his heart" that can help us to understand unique personal qualities that are as relevant at the onset of the twenty-first century as they were when Nelson crowned his achievements and died at Trafalgar in 1805.

Acknowledgments

I am deeply grateful to Colin White, Deputy Director of the Royal Naval Museum and a respected Nelson author, who reviewed the manuscript for this book and provided extremely important insights and suggestions. Also, I wish to acknowledge the help of that special group of people who recognize the relevance of Nelson's life to present-day issues. Particularly, I thank Captain Ira Dye, USN (retired), for his invaluable comments and Dr. James Tritten, who generously contributed to my understanding of Nelson's character. The creative talents of Terry Weckbaugh at Image Quest Photographic Studio were an important enabling factor in reproducing the rare illustrations that nourish Nelson's words. I thank Karen Doody for her outstanding cover and book designs. Finally, the manuscript for *Nelson Speaks* was edited by Kimberley VanDerveer and Chris Findlay with skill and patience; their efforts are sincerely appreciated.

Chronology

1758

29 Sept.   Born at Burnham Thorpe Parsonage in Norfolk. Author Tom Pocock described the powerful sea orientation of that salt-air-scoured English coast in his book, *Nelson and His World:* "When northerly gales blow from the sea, the beech trees above Burnham Thorpe heel and roll like masts. When the wind drops, the murmur of surf can be heard from the Norfolk shore." In the small waters along that Norfolk coast, Nelson began developing the special combination of blue water and in-shore seamanship that was to be an important factor in his historic naval career.

1767

26 Dec.   Catherine, Nelson's mother, died. By all accounts, including his own, he was very close to her. Her death undoubtedly left deep and permanent marks on his character. One was his "susceptible heart," a quality that was to have a powerful influence on both his personal life and his professional career. In sharp contrast was an

abiding hatred of the French, which began with his mother's strong anti-French feelings.

1770

27 Nov.   Appointed midshipman at age twelve, and reported aboard HMS *Raisonnable,* commanded by his uncle Maurice Suckling. According to Nelson biographers M'Arthur and Clarke, when Nelson's father, Edmund, asked Suckling to take his son to sea as a midshipman, Suckling responded: "What has poor Horace (Nelson's preferred nickname as a small boy) done, who is so weak, that he, above all the rest, should be sent to rough it out at sea? But let him come and the first time we go into action a cannon ball may knock off his head and provide for him at once."

1771

Aug.   Shipped aboard a merchantman to the West Indies. His experience in the merchant service was not unusual for British naval officers when they were between naval assignments, and it gave him a broadened perspective on life at sea and the skills it demanded. Those seaman's skills were to play an important—at times underrecognized—role in his career. His experience in the merchant marine also contributed to an appreciation for the abilities of the ordinary seaman, something not all British naval officers of the time shared.

1772

July   Returned to England.

1773

Mar.   Appointed midshipman aboard HMS *Seahorse* and sailed for the East Indies, adding knowledge of the waters of that area to his experience in the West Indies and Arctic Ocean.

June   Joined an expedition in search of an Arctic route to the Pacific. This experience further broadened Nelson's knowledge of the sea and of seamen.

1775

19 Feb.   Experienced combat for the first time. This eng... off the coast of India, between *Seahorse* and a local ... of the French, was Nelson's initial experience with the battle efficiency of a well-trained British navy crew and a hard-fought victory at sea.

Dec.   Fell ill from malaria, a disease that probably contributed to his many health problems over the course of his life.

1776

Mar.   Sailed for England as a patient in HMS *Dolphin*. During this voyage he came close to dying. Following a period of deep depression about his career prospects, a spiritual experience convinced him that he would become a hero in the service of his king and country.

Sept.   Appointed acting lieutenant aboard HMS *Worcester*.

1777

9 Apr.   Received permanent promotion to lieutenant and assigned to HMS *Lowestoffe* for duty in the West Indies. The ship's captain, William Locker, made a strong impression on the young lieutenant and became a lifelong friend whom Nelson considered a mentor. In later years, Nelson would acknowledge Locker's influence with specificity: "[I]t was you who always told me, 'Lay a Frenchman close, and you will beat him.'"

1778

Sept.   Appointed first lieutenant in HMS *Bristol*.

Dec.   Appointed to his first command, HMS *Badger*. This tour of duty gets only one paragraph in his own "Sketch of My Life," and generally little discussion among his biographers, but anyone who has gone to sea knows that it had to be a defining experience for the future admiral and peerless hero.

1779

11 June   Appointed post captain at twenty years of age, and appointed to command HMS *Hinchinbrooke*.

naval portion of an unsuccessful
ʃuan in Nicaragua, the first of many
ʃed joint efforts with the British army.
ration he demonstrated the exceptional
that distinguished him in future military

d to command of HMS *Janus* and suffered
a major illness, presumably a recurrence of
a, one of many physical challenges he overcame
ʃ ʃng his career.

Dec.   Returned to England.

1781

Aug.   Appointed to command of HMS *Albemarle.* Conducted merchant ship convoy duty in the Baltic, again extending his geographic experience.

1782

Nov.   Served in Lord Hood's squadron operating off the northeast coast of North America and Canada, adding still another operational area to his experience. Returned to the West Indies.

1783

Mar.   Failed in attack on Turks Island in the West Indies. This failure presaged other failures later in his career at Santa Cruz in the Canary Islands and at Boulogne, France.

June   Returned to England.

Oct.   Began a four-month visit to St. Omer, France.

1784

Mar.   Appointed to command of HMS *Boreas,* and sailed for the West Indies.

1785

May   Met his future wife, Frances Nisbet, a young widow in Nevis, West Indies, where she lived with her son. Nelson's early letters to his wife are a dramatic demonstration of his emotional side. They also are extremely poignant in light of the unhappy ending of his relationship with his wife and notorious romance with Emma Lady Hamilton.

1786

Nov.   Began a brief assignment as aide to Prince William Henry, Duke of Clarence and later King William IV. This relationship was to continue throughout Nelson's life.

1787

Mar.   Married Frances Nisbet in Nevis.

July   Returned with his wife, Fanny, to Burnham Thorpe, where Nelson remained on half pay without a navy assignment.

1793

Jan.   Appointed to command HMS *Agamemnon.*

Feb.   War between Britain and France renewed.

June   Sailed for the Mediterranean and blockade duty off Toulon.

Sept.   Met Lord and Lady Hamilton in Naples, where Lord Hamilton was Ambassador to the Kingdom of the Two Sicilies.

1794

Jan.   Corsican naval campaign began. During the campaign, flying debris thrown up by a cannon shot injured Nelson's right eye and, as a result of the injury, he lost the sight of the eye. (Some representations inaccurately depict Nelson wearing a patch over his right eye. At times he did wear an eye shade over his left eye, which over time became increasingly sensitive to strong light.)

1795

Mar.   Distinguished himself in action off Genoa against the French ship, *Ça Ira.*

1796

Mar.   Appointed commodore. At this point, Nelson began his career as a superb leader of fleet units in combat.

May   Transferred to HMS *Captain.*

1797

14 Feb.   Took part in the Battle of Cape St. Vincent. This event catapulted Nelson into broad public attention. That process was aided by some skillful letter writing on his part, an effort that precipitated dramatic newspaper accounts of his professional ability and bravery. As a result of his achievements at Cape St. Vincent, he was created Knight of the Bath. Six days after the battle, he was promoted to rear admiral on the basis of seniority.

July   Led boat actions off Cadiz harbor involving hand-to-hand combat.

24 July   Led a disastrous amphibious assault on Santa Cruz, Tenerife. The Spanish army and militia forces, led by a tough and resourceful Castillian general, Antonio Gutiérrez, inflicted heavy casualties on the British. During the attack Nelson's right arm was wounded and quickly amputated. The aftermath of the battle was a classic example of the professional respect that opposing professional warriors frequently have for one another. With his confidence badly shaken, Nelson returned to England where he was nursed by Lady Nelson and recovered from his defeat and wound.

1798

Mar.   Hoisted his rear admiral's flag in HMS *Vanguard* and joined the fleet commanded by Admiral Sir John Jervis, by then Earl St. Vincent, off Cadiz. Nelson was selected over more senior admirals for an independent Mediterranean command with the mission to locate and destroy a French invasion fleet with Napoleon embarked.

1 Aug.   Located the French battle fleet in Aboukir Bay just east of Alexandria, Egypt, after a nerve-racking, crisscrossing search of the eastern Mediterranean. He destroyed all but two of the thirteen French ships of the line, utilizing the aggressive tactics for which he became famous. He received a head wound that included a serious laceration and a concussion. His refusal to take precedence over oth-

ers being attended by the ship's surgeon added to his reputation among his crew. The concussion's aftermath caused him continuing physical problems.

22 Sept. Returned to Naples to a welcome that reached hysterical proportions. Following the Battle of the Nile, Nelson's attention focused on supporting the Kingdom of the Two Sicilies against French military pressure. During this period, his romance with Lady Hamilton began, and many at the Admiralty and Whitehall developed serious concerns about the impact of that relationship on his professional judgment.

Nov. Created Baron Nelson of the Nile as a result of his extraordinary victory at the Battle of the Nile.

Dec. Rescued the royal family of the Kingdom of the Two Sicilies from French troops approaching Naples. Moved the Neapolitan Court, plus Lord and Lady Hamilton, to Palermo from Naples.

1799

June Returned to Naples as the French were abandoning that city. One of his first actions was to cancel a treaty between the Neapolitan Royalists and the remnants of the French army and local rebels. Nelson's approval of the summary execution of Admiral Caracciolo during this period—and the dumping of Caracciolo's body into the harbor—became a source of criticism of his actions during this time.

July Disobeyed orders from his commander in chief, Admiral Lord Keith, to sail to Minorca in order to remain in Palermo. At the time, Palermo was the temporary location of the court of the Kingdom of the Two Sicilies and of Lady Hamilton.

Aug. Created Duke of Bronte by the King of the Kingdom of the Two Sicilies.

1800

Feb. Captured *LeGenéréux,* one of the only two French ships of the line that escaped after the Battle of the Nile.

July	Began return home overland in the company of Lord and Lady Hamilton and further fueled the scandal over his love affair with Lady Hamilton.

1801

1 Jan.	Promoted to vice admiral.
Jan.	Separated from Lady Nelson.
Jan.	Hoisted his flag in HMS *San Josef.*
1 Feb.	Horatia, daughter of Nelson and Lady Hamilton, was born.
Mar.	Departed for the Baltic under the command of Admiral Sir Hyde Parker.
2 Apr.	Led the attacking British squadron in the Battle of Copenhagen. At the height of the battle, he disregarded the signal to withdraw made by Hyde Parker. He pressed on until victory was in hand, and then, in tough truce negotiations, he achieved an important strategic victory for Britain.
May	Created Viscount Nelson of the Nile and Burnham Thorpe.
Aug.	Was in overall command of an unsuccessful attack on a portion of a French invasion force assembled at Boulogne.
1 Oct.	France and Britain signed an armistice.
22 Oct.	Joined Lord and Lady Hamilton at Merton, a home he purchased for himself and the Hamiltons.

1802

27 Mar.	Britain and France agreed to the Treaty of Amiens.

1803

16 May	War between Britain and France renewed.
18 May	Hoisted his flag in HMS *Victory* (now preserved as a national treasure at the Historic Dockyard, Portsmouth) as commander in chief in the Mediterranean. In July, he joined the British fleet off Toulon, and in the following months he maintained a blockade of Toulon that was intended to lure the French fleet into action. This duty was one of many blockades that tested the men and

ships of the British navy during the ongoing conflict with Napoleon.

Aug.   French mounted preparations to invade Britain.
1804

Dec.   War declared by Spain against Britain.
1805

Apr.–   Chased the French fleet, led by Admiral Villeneuve, to
July   the West Indies and back. Villeneuve, in a matter of months, became his opponent at the Battle of Trafalgar.

Aug.–   Returned to England for his last leave at Merton.
Sept.

14 Sept.   Rejoined HMS *Victory* and, two weeks later, took command of the British fleet off Cadiz.

21 Oct.   Led British fleet in the Battle of Trafalgar. Once again, he employed aggressive tactics, in this case against a combined French and Spanish fleet. This battle was a prime example of Nelson's thorough briefing of his captains and his reliance on the fighting superiority of the British navy's seamen in close combat at sea. During the battle he was mortally wounded by a French sniper's bullet and died several hours later. The victory energized Britain at a crucial time in its struggle with Napoleon.

1806

9 Jan.   Buried in St. Paul's Cathedral directly under the great dome. The funeral was a spectacle of unique dimensions. In her biography of Nelson, Carola Oman described one of the unusual features of the crowd that lined the funeral route. She wrote, "[T]he only general sound made by an unusually orderly mob was one resembling a murmur of the sea, caused by a spontaneous movement to uncover as the funeral car came in sight."

Nelson Speaks

"I hold my duty as I hold my soul."
—Shakespeare

1. Duty

~

"Whilst I have the honour to command an English Man-of-War, I never shall allow myself to be subservient to the will of any Governor, nor co-operate with him in doing illegal acts."
Written from HMS *Boreas* to Rear Admiral Sir Richard Hughes, January 1785

One of the defining periods in Nelson's early career was his assignment as commanding officer of HMS *Boreas* at age twenty-five in the West Indies. During that tour he demonstrated a stubborn determination to carry out his duty, as he saw it, even if it required him to oppose his seniors. As commanding officer of *Boreas* he refused to wink at violations of Britain's Navigation Acts,[1] which forbade trade between the former American colonies and British possessions in the Caribbean. Britain's West Indian administrators and business leaders were more interested in lucrative trading than in obeying the legislation, enacted at a distance, to protect Britain's commerce and industries. As a result, they consistently found ways to circumvent the Navigation Acts.

Nelson embarrassed and enraged the local administrators and traders by scrupulously enforcing the Acts. This insistence on doing his duty caused him serious legal problems, and could have cost him his career. Fortunately for Britain, he survived the legal actions brought against him, and the Admiralty, after considerable delay, affirmed the correctness of his actions in the West Indies. The final legal outcome of Nelson's insistence on enforcement of the Navigation Acts was an early reinforcement of his conviction that he himself was the ultimate determiner of what constituted his duty.

"I stand for myself; no great connexion to support me if inclined to fall: therefore my good Name as a Man, and Officer, and an Englishman, I must be very careful of. My greatest pride is to discharge my duty faithfully; my greatest ambition to receive approbation for my conduct."

Written from HMS *Boreas* to Lord Sydney,
British Secretary of State, March 1785

As a young post captain, Nelson was not reluctant to lecture his civilian leaders in Whitehall. His emphasis on not only doing his duty but wanting to be recognized for it, showed that he had insights into his own personality. His mention of having "no great connexion" refers to the then-system in the British navy whereby critical appointments were frequently based on influence—referred to as "interest"—from high places. In fact, initially Nelson had significant interest through his uncle Maurice Suckling, who died in 1778.

❧

"Are not the King's Ships here employed to see the Navigation Act and the King's Order of Council carried into effect?"
Written from HMS *Boreas* to his uncle
William Suckling, November 1785

Even after a year of legal problems that threatened his career, and extensive social ostracism that kept him aboard his ship while in port, Nelson continued doggedly to focus on what he clearly saw as his duty.

❧

"Duty is the great business of a Sea Officer. All private considerations must give way to it, however Painful it is."
Written from HMS *Boreas* to Frances Nisbet,
his future wife, May 1786

Although he courted Frances Nisbet ardently, frequently proclaiming his love and respect for her in emotional terms, Nelson nevertheless saw fit to lecture his bride-to-be on the primacy of his naval duty. These lines, in their very personal context, underscore his extremely strong sense of duty to his country, a personal quality that continued to be a major driving force throughout his entire naval career.

❧

"Our Country has the first demand for our services; and private convenience, or happiness, must ever give way to the Public good."
Written from HMS *Boreas* to his future wife,
December 1786

Nelson's continued emphasis on his duty to his country was one precursor of trouble in his marriage. In later years that sense of duty, in conflict with Fanny's failure to better understand that part of his character, was a factor—but not the only one—in the demise of their relationship.

≈

"It is very true that I have ever served faithfully, and ever has it been my fate to be neglected; but that shall not make me inattentive to my duty."

Written from HMS *Agamemnon* to his wife,
January 1795

Many of Nelson's detractors point out accurately that he had a compelling drive for glory, often reflected in his complaints that he did not get full credit for some of his achievements, particularly the victory at Copenhagen in 1801. One of the manifestations of this belief was that, at times, he turned self-publicist. A striking example of this was his successful effort, a few years after this letter and following the Battle of Cape St. Vincent in 1797, to have his remarkable combat accomplishments publicly recognized in Britain. However, when all was said and done, Nelson's powerful sense of duty more than matched his need for glory, and it sustained him when public approbation was lacking.

≈

"God forbid, I should have any other consideration on service, than the good of my Country."

Written from Leghorn to his wife,
February 1796

This allusion to God in connection with duty, although seemingly casual, was not meaningless for Nelson. Deep religious feelings were an important underpinning of his sense of duty. From his earliest writings to his last, his belief that "God was on his side" was continually in evidence.

～

"[I]t will be credited, if my character is known, that this block-ade will be attended to with a degree of rigour unexampled in the present war."

Written from HMS *Captain* to Joseph Brame,
British Consul at Genoa, July 1796

During Britain's wars with Revolutionary and Napoleonic France, arduous and grinding sea blockades were among the most telling weapons Britain wielded against the French. Although Nelson was strongly impelled towards offensive attack, he realized that these blockades were essential elements in an effective naval strategy against the French. He accepted them as important, if onerous, duty, and pursued them with a tenacity that was typical of the British navy of his time.

～

"I would have every man believe, I shall only take my chance of being shot by the Enemy, but if I do not take that chance, I am certain of being shot by my Friends."

Written from Bath to Captain Albemarle Bertie,
January 1798

Bravery under fire was one of Nelson's most important leadership qualities, and he was not beyond introducing some wry humor to the dangers of combat. His coolness under fire was clearly evident at the battles of Cape St. Vincent, Santa Cruz, the Nile, Copenhagen, Trafalgar, and a number of other potentially lethal but less epic engagements. He had a fatalistic approach to mortal danger, and his very visible courage under fire was one of the reasons he inspired unusual loyalty in his officers and men.

❦

"You will easily conceive my feelings at the order this day received here from Lord Keith; but my mind, your Lordship will know . . . was fully prepared for this order; and more than ever is my mind made up, that, at this moment, I will not part with a single Ship, as I cannot do that without drawing a hundred and twenty men from each Ship now at the Siege of Capua, where an Army is gone this day. I am fully aware of the act I have committed; but sensible of my loyal intentions, I am prepared for any fate which may await my disobedience. . . . I have done what I thought right; others may think differently; but it will be my consolation that I have gained a Kingdom, seated a faithful Ally of His Majesty firmly on his throne, and restored happiness to millions. Do not think, my dear Lord, that my opinion is formed from the arrangements of anyone. No; be it good, or be it bad, it is all my own."

Written from HMS *Foudroyant* to Earl Spencer,
First Lord of the Admiralty, July 1799

For any other admiral in the British navy, this letter would almost certainly have marked the end of his career. Nelson had not only refused the order of his commander in chief to detach some of his ships to Minorca, he also went over his chief's head to the First Lord of the Admiralty. However, while Nelson's commander in chief, Lord Keith, was understandably exasperated and outraged, Earl Spencer and others, like Earl St. Vincent, placed Nelson's combat ability over his propensity for departing from the orders of his seniors.

Two additional points emerge from these lines to Spencer. The first is that, despite the assumption by many that Nelson's refusal of orders was intolerable, his strategic assessment of the paramount importance of his preserving the Two Sicilies as a viable ally of Britain may well have been correct. The second point is that Nelson was clearly aware of the fact that there were many at the Admiralty and Whitehall who believed that he was being unduly influenced by Lady Hamilton.

~

"I certainly, from only having a left hand, cannot enter into details which may explain the motives which actuate my conduct, and which may be necessary for a Commanding officer, who may wish to have every subject of duty detailed by those under his command. My principle, my dear Lord, is to assist in driving the French to the Devil, and in restoring peace and happiness to mankind. I feel I am fitter to do the action than to describe it."

Written from Naples to Earl Spencer,
First Lord of the Admiralty, August 1799

This apparently impertinent and typically Nelsonian statement illuminates how Nelson often defined his duty in terms of his hatred of the French. He believed that he was fighting a dangerous anti-Christian, antimonarchical movement, personified in Napoleon. To him, the conflicts with the French went beyond protection of Britain's empire and commerce. In blunt terms, Nelson emphasized his focus on actions that advanced Britain's military objectives against its arch foe rather than on correspondence with his civilian leaders at the Admiralty. He also managed to include reference to his loss of an arm in combat, a gambit he was to use on occasion in his correspondence to emphasize his sacrifices for Britain.

~

"[I]t was needless for your Excellency to lay such a stress to remind me of what, I dare say, you thought the duty of a

British Admiral. I am not accustomed to be wanting in the service of our King."

Written from Palermo to William Wyndham,
British Minister at Florence, October 1799

Gratuitous advice was not appreciated from most deskbound officials in Whitehall, and Nelson did not hesitate to make that abundantly clear on occasion. To a significant degree, he considered the civilians at Whitehall and the Admiralty to be rear-echelon nuisances.

❧

"[T]he General would not, on any consideration, break his orders for any object. . . . Much as I approve the strict obedience to orders—even to a Court-Martial to inquire whether the object justified the measure—yet to say that an Officer is never, for any object, to alter his orders, is what I cannot comprehend. The circumstances of this war so often vary, that an Officer has almost every moment to consider—What would my superiors direct, did they know what is passing under my nose?"

Written from Palermo to Earl Spencer,
First Lord of the Admiralty, November 1799

At times Nelson was frustrated by his inability to get the British army to join in a combined action that he believed would advance Britain's cause against the French. In this instance it was his hope to recapture Malta. His request to General Sir James St. Clair that he and his regiment join in the action was refused because the regiment had been ordered back to England and was awaiting its relief. Although Nelson participated in numerous joint army-navy operations without rancor—such as the successful evacuation of Bastia in 1796—at times he could be sharply critical of the army's perceived lack of initiative.

The use of the term "alter his orders" is interesting and suggests that Nelson thought of his noteworthy departures from orders as *alterations* toward realizing the larger objectives rather than as disobedience. Admiral Earl St. Vincent agreed with Nelson's approach when St. Vincent was the fleet commander at the Battle of Cape St. Vincent and, later, when he served in the Admiralty as its First Lord. Others, like then–Captain Robert Calder at Cape St. Vincent, felt that Nelson was a threat to good order and discipline in the British navy.

Nelson's statement about trying to carry out what would be the orders of his superiors, if they were on the scene at the time of the events, also is interesting. By suggesting that he would be trying to carry out the will of his seniors if they only knew the facts—a neat twist of logic—he almost surely intended to make this letter less defiant. Whether or not Nelson's political superiors paid much attention to his argument, it was very much in their interest to overlook his contentiousness. They placed him in key roles and he rewarded them with key victories.

"I find that few think as I do—but to obey orders is all perfection! To serve my King and destroy the French, I consider as the great order of all, from which little ones spring; and if one of these little ones militate against it, (for, who can tell exactly at a distance?) I go back to obey the great order and object, and down, down with the damned French villains."

Written from HMS *Vanguard* to the
Duke of Clarence, November 1799

Nelson's approach to interpreting his orders made many at the Admiralty nervous. His willingness to make his own decisions—at times in contravention to orders from his distant seniors—was not always appreciated. However, Nelson had an uncanny ability to grasp both strategic and tactical situations, and he repeatedly risked his career to do the right thing based on both the situation at hand and his overall mission.

Fortunately, there were seniors like Admiral Earl St. Vincent who recognized Nelson's unique value as a warrior, and who placed him in positions of combat command in crucial situations. Such confidence in Nelson's abilities resulted in the British navy's historically critical victories at the battles of the Nile in 1798, Copenhagen in 1801, and Trafalgar in 1805.

❧

"You have, my friend, gained more honour by obeying my order against that of your Prince, and for which His Royal Highness will thank you, than ever can be done by obedience, if it is to injure the good Cause."

Written from Palermo to the Marquis De Niza,
Portuguese admiral, November 1799

After the Battle of the Nile, the Marquis De Niza led a Portuguese squadron under Nelson's command. Nelson assigned the blockade of Malta—occupied by Napoleon on his way to Egypt in 1798—to the Marquis. After the Portuguese government ordered De Niza back to Lisbon, Nelson exerted extremely strong pressure on him to remain on station to prevent the relief of the occupying French forces. Eventually Malta was freed of its French occupiers, thanks in significant part to the willingness of the Marquis to remain on station after his government ordered him home.

High regard for Britain's allies was not often reflected in Nelson's statements. To the contrary, his comments about them were frequently caustic. The thanks expressed by Nelson in his letter to De Niza was another example of his belief that obedience to orders was contingent upon meeting an overall military objective.

"Do you know what's shown on board of the Commander-in-Chief? Why, to leave off Action! Now damn me if I do. You know, Foley, I have only one eye—I have a right to be blind sometimes. [Placing his long glass to his blind eye] I really do not see the signal."

Attributed to Nelson at the Battle of Copenhagen,
2 April 1801, by then–Colonel The Honorable
William Stewart who was present, July 1801

Nelson's coolness under fire was never more evident than at the fiercely fought Battle of Copenhagen. In that instance, he tempered his departure from orders signaled from his commander-in-chief, Admiral Sir Hyde Parker, with self-mocking humor that alluded to one of his previous battle wounds.

After Nelson's victory at Copenhagen, Hyde Parker was relieved and Nelson was placed in command of Britain's Baltic Fleet. As a result of the victory at Copenhagen and the death of the Tsar, the circumstances that precipitated the British attack on Copenhagen were mitigated. And Britain secured an important strategic victory.

"At this distance it is impossible for me to regulate every thing with exactness. . . . We must all in our several stations exert ourselves to the utmost, and not be nonsensical in saying, 'I have an order for this, that, or the other,' if the King's service clearly marks what ought to be done."

Written from HMS *Victory* to Captain Schomberg
of HMS *Madras*, October 1803

In dealing with the captains of ships under his command, Nelson established the same guidelines that he sought with his seniors: use your initiative to do the right thing under the existing circumstances; he preached what he practiced.

Overcoming the Danes in the fiercely fought Battle of Copenhagen was the means of achieving important strategic objectives in the Baltic for Britain. *The Battle of Copenhagen, April 2, 1801*; engraving by J. Fittler, from a painting by Nicholas Pocock.

"With respect to my making War upon Spain, and Sir John Orde not having done it, I believe you will think that I have acted not precipitately, but consistent with the firmness of John Bull. I can't tell what schemes Ministers may have; but when I am without orders, and unexpected occurrences arise, I shall always act as I think the honour and glory of my King and Country demand."

Written from HMS *Victory* to Hugh Elliot,
British Ambassador at Naples, January 1805

At one point, Sir John Orde was given a command in an area of operation off Cadiz, adjacent to Nelson's Mediterranean command. Nelson resented it on two counts. First, he thought the command should have been given to someone junior to himself, an officer who would report to him. Instead Orde, who was senior to Nelson, was given the command, an assignment with considerable potential for prize money. And that potential for prize money was Nelson's second problem.

For Orde's part, he resented Nelson having the prestigious Mediterranean command for which he believed he was more deserving on the basis of his seniority. Nelson, with obvious bitterness, got past the conflict by focusing on his duty, the foundation that supported his career.

"I hope my absence will not be long, and that I shall soon meet the Combined Fleets, with a force sufficient to do the job well; for half a Victory would but half content me."

Written from Merton to Alexander Davison,
his friend and agent, September 1805

There was nothing halfway in Nelson's sense of duty. He understood that Britain's national strategy required total victory over the Combined Fleet of France and Spain. This was particularly noteworthy since, before Nelson's time, marginal victories or standoffs were the most common results of sea battles.

～

"But, in case Signals can neither be seen or perfectly understood, no Captain can do very wrong if he places his ship alongside that of an Enemy."

Written from HMS *Victory* in a memo to his captains,
October 1805

Nelson gave his captains the same latitude he expected from his seniors. In his instructions to his captains before the Battle of Trafalgar, he established a combat doctrine that was completely consistent with his own actions. He believed strongly that individual captains must have the flexibility to react to opportunities and the circumstances of the moment in battle, and he had repeatedly departed from his seniors' orders to capitalize on the unpredictable events of combat at sea. On the eve of Trafalgar, he made it clear to his captains, often referred to as his Band of Brothers, that their ultimate duty was to use their initiative to reach the overall objective—total victory.[2]

～

"England expects that every man will do his duty."

Signal from Nelson aboard HMS *Victory* to his fleet
at the beginning of the Battle of Trafalgar,
October 1805

At Trafalgar, Nelson had supreme confidence in the skills of his captains and their crews. His last signal to, as he put it, "amuse the fleet" indicated that he also had confidence in their sense of duty. The now-famous nine-word message was straight-forward. It put the emphasis on doing one's duty, and also suggested that Nelson had full confidence in every British sailor's own sense of duty.

One of the interesting side notes about this signal is that, in Nelson's original order to his signal officer, he used the word "confides" instead of "expects." The latter was substituted for "confides" because it made for a shorter flag signal.

"Thank God I have done my duty."
> Attributed to Nelson by Dr. William Beatty, surgeon
> aboard HMS *Victory* at the Battle of Trafalgar,
> 21 October 1805

As Nelson was dying, he learned that he had achieved a great victory for the British at Trafalgar. During the hours he lay wounded in *Victory*'s cockpit, he spoke of the need for an overwhelming victory, as well as his concern for the future of his paramour, Lady Hamilton, and their daughter, Horatia. He also showed concern to his flag captain and friend, Thomas Hardy, about the storm he knew was coming.

But his choice of last words vividly underscores the depth of his commitment to his duty and how that commitment anchored his brilliant career.

> "Even the bravest cannot fight
> beyond his strength."
> —Homer

2. Toughness

~

*"Our loss has been trifling, not twenty killed and wounded:
amongst the former is Captain Serocold, and amongst the latter, in a slight manner, is myself, my head being a good deal
wounded, and my right eye cut down; but the Surgeons flatter me I shall not entirely lose the sight, which I believe, for I
can already distinguish light from dark. It confined me, thank
God, only one day, and at a time when nothing particular
happened to be doing."*

Written from Calvi, Corsica, to Sir Gilbert Elliot,
British Viceroy at Corsica, July 1794

Although Nelson was not a physically imposing man, he demonstrated exceptional physical toughness when wounded. During an
action on Corsica against the French, he was involved in setting
up artillery batteries ashore. At one point, a round shot fired by
the enemy struck the earthen works near him, and the gravel
flung up by the impact struck him in the right eye. Although he

made light of the wound in his correspondence with his wife and others, the injury at Calvi—plus other eye problems probably caused by continuous exposure to bright sunlight—cost him the sight of that eye. In addition, his left eye increasingly grew painful to bright light throughout the rest of his life, and he often wore a small shade over his forehead—not an eye patch as sometimes depicted—to reduce bright light.

As with his other wounds, the eye injury was a source of humor for Nelson. He described the fact that the eye and his face were not disfigured: "So my *beauty* is saved." As a further demonstration of his toughness he noted that, conveniently, the wound was followed by a day that wasn't very busy!

"I am sorry that you should have to differ with Vice Admiral Thompson but had it been Christmas Day instead of Sunday, I would have executed them."
Written from HMS *Theseus* to Captain Sir Robert Calder,
flag captain to Admiral Earl St. Vincent, July 1797

In 1797 there were serious mutinies in the British navy.[1] By then Earl St. Vincent was the admiral in command of the Mediterranean Fleet and, when confronted with a potential mutiny, St. Vincent acted swiftly. The mutineers were quickly tried and convicted in the instance to which Nelson referred. However, because their trials ended after sundown, they could not be executed the same day, which was the admiral's original intention. However, he did hang the mutineers on the following day, a Sunday, despite the practice in the British navy of not administering capital punishment on the Sabbath. St. Vincent's unusual action was publicly criticized by Vice Admiral Thompson, and Nelson's unequivocal agreement with his senior's swift punishment reflected his own tough-minded attitude that certain crimes like mutiny must be dealt with swiftly, severely, and publicly.

It also is interesting to note that by this time St. Vincent had become an important role model for Nelson. And progressively, St. Vincent was to become one of his strongest supporters at the Admiralty and Whitehall.

~

"Let me alone, I have yet my legs left, and one arm. Tell the surgeon to make haste and get his instruments. I know I must lose my right arm, so the sooner it is off the better."

Attributed to Nelson, from an account of the aftermath of the Battle of Santa Cruz in the *London Gazette,* 24 July 1797

One result of Nelson's disastrously unsuccessful attack on Santa Cruz on the Island of Tenerife was the wound he suffered during the assault. As he stepped ashore in the face of withering fire from the town's defenders, his right arm was shattered above the elbow. The British attribute the wound to a musket shot; the Spanish attribute it to grape shot from a cannon they referred to as "El Tigre," which today is displayed in the Museo Militar in Santa Cruz.

When he was returned to his flagship, HMS *Theseus,* Nelson refused assistance in getting up the ship's side. One observer described the ascent, which can be difficult even under normal circumstances. He told how Nelson approached the ship with "his right arm dangling by his side, whilst with his left he jumped up the ship's side, and displayed a spirit that astonished every one."

Nelson's arm quickly was amputated without anesthetic. Within a half hour, he reportedly was giving orders almost as if nothing had happened. Nelson's response to his wound and amputation was another striking demonstration of both his physical and mental toughness.

Nelson's stepson, Josiah Nisbet, undoubtedly saved his stepfather's life by returning Nelson to his flagship where his shattered right arm was amputated without anesthetic. *Sir Horatio Nelson when Wounded at Teneriffe, Night of July 24, 1797;* engraving by J. Naegle, from a painting by Richard Westall.

~

*"I beg neither you or my father will think much of this mishap:
my mind has long been made up to such an event."*
Written from HMS *Theseus* to his wife, August 1797

After Nelson's right arm was shattered and amputated at the
Battle of Santa Cruz, he wrote to Fanny saying that she and
Nelson's father shouldn't think much of his wound. His statement about being resigned to battle injuries was one of many
fatalistic comments about his personal well-being in battle. The
attitude that his personal safety was beyond his control had a lot
to do with his fearless behavior in combat.

~

"I will take my turn with my brave followers."
Attributed to Nelson by Captain Edward Berry,
flag captain aboard HMS *Vanguard* at the
Battle of the Nile, 1 August 1798

Nelson was seriously wounded at the Battle of the Nile when he
was struck in the head by langrage,[2] a piece of jagged metal shot
used to damage the opponent's rigging and to kill or injure personnel on deck. The surgeon moved immediately to attend to
Nelson when he was brought below to the ship's cockpit, where
the wounded were being treated. But Nelson insisted that those
who were waiting for treatment before him be attended to first.
This fusion of courage and consideration was not only a demonstration of his physical toughness but was the kind of behavior
that inspired fierce loyalty among the seamen he commanded.

~

*"My head is so upset, that really I know not what to do; but
by to-morrow morning I will arrange matters in my mind,
and do my best."*
Written from HMS *Vanguard* to Admiral Earl St. Vincent,
August 1798

Although the bloody laceration to his head was what drew the attention of Nelson and those around him at the Battle of the Nile, it was what is now presumed to have been a serious concussion that was the more significant wound. When this letter was written two weeks after the battle, he was still suffering the effects of that concussion. And, despite Nelson's prediction, those effects were to continue well beyond the day after this letter was written. However, he somehow managed to endure and overcome his troubling combination of physical and mental difficulties.

~

"[S]peedy rewards and quick punishments are the foundation of good government."
Written from Palermo to Captain Thomas Troubridge,
HMS *Culloden,* March 1799

Troubridge was a friend and trusted subordinate of Nelson's. On 28 March 1799, Nelson ordered him to blockade Naples, then in the control of the French, and the adjacent coast of Italy with a detached squadron. At that point Nelson had evacuated the Royal Family of the Kingdom of the Two Sicilies from Naples to Palermo. After the evacuation, Nelson remained in Palermo in close proximity to his paramour, Lady Hamilton. Troubridge's assignment included efforts to retake several small islands in the harbor of Naples and to support efforts by local Royalist forces to "take arms to liberate their Country from French tyranny."

Two days after the dispatch containing his initial orders to Troubridge, Nelson sent a second dispatch with parallel orders from the King of the Kingdom of the Two Sicilies. Nelson used the latter orders to provide Troubridge with the benefit of the eleven-word theory of good government contained in this letter. It was typical of the no nonsense, sometimes harsh, side of Nelson's personality. To some observers, this part of Nelson's persona appeared to be particularly evident during 1799, a period when his critics believed him to be inordinately influenced by Lady Hamilton.

❧

"Send me word some proper heads are taken off: this alone will comfort me."

Written from Palermo to Captain Thomas Troubridge,
HMS *Culloden,* April 1799

Troubridge's mission succeeded in gaining control of the islands in the Bay of Naples; in the process, local officials who had cooperated with the French were captured. Nelson is brutally explicit at this point about what he meant by the "quick punishments" he had mentioned to Troubridge in his dispatch of a few weeks earlier.

❧

"It is now my duty to speak out, and not to be misunderstood. That Nelson who has hitherto kept your powerful Enemies from destroying you, can, and will, let them loose upon you, unless the following terms are, in two hours, complied with."

Written from HMS *Vanguard* to the Bashaw of Tripoli,
April 1799

Like many British navy officers of his time, Nelson was called upon to deal with diplomatic situations. His approach to an ongoing and troublesome relationship with the Bashaw of Tripoli reflects his technique of relying on undisguised threats, only lightly seasoned with reasoned argument.

❧

"I have not been able to pay that attention to the Barbary States I could have wished: but I know these folks must be talked to with honesty and firmness."

Written from Palermo to Admiral Earl St. Vincent,
June 1799

Although Nelson took a tough approach with the Muslim leaders of the Mediterranean, his recognition that honesty must be a part of his dealings with them arguably set him apart from many of the career diplomats who were his contemporaries.

～

"Your news of the hanging of thirteen Jacobins gave us great pleasure; and the three Priests, I hope, return in the Aurora, to dangle on the tree best adapted to their weight of sins."
Written from Palermo to Captain Edward Foote,
HMS *Seahorse,* June 1799

During 1799 Nelson defied orders to give up his proximity to the court of the Kingdom of the Two Sicilies and Lady Hamilton. He claimed that his protection of the Two Sicilies was of overriding importance; many believed it was his attachment to Lady Hamilton that was his driving motivation. It also was a time when he showed the hard streak in his nature. Even his humor seemed to have an excessively hard edge.

～

"[V]ictories cannot be obtained without blood."
Written from Palermo to Captain Edward Foote,
HMS *Seahorse,* June 1799

Nelson accepted his numerous wounds as a normal consequence of battle. He was equally tough about combat casualties in general, and this attitude clearly was a part of both his battle doctrine and his tactics. For him, combat casualties were the inevitable price of the victories that he was convinced were absolutely necessary for Britain.

~

"You are hereby required and directed to cause the said sentence of death to be carried into execution upon the said Francisco Caracciolo accordingly, by hanging him at the fore yard-arm of His Sicilian Majesty's Frigate La Minerva, under your command, at five o'clock this evening; and to cause him to hang there until sunset, when you will have his body cut down, and thrown into the sea."

Written from HMS *Foudroyant* in Naples Bay to
Commodore Count Thurn, Commander of
His Sicilian Majesty's Frigate, *La Minerva,* June 1799

The manner of the execution of Francisco Caracciolo has been a source of criticism of Nelson. Caracciolo undoubtedly had cooperated with the French forces occupying Naples, and was considered by the King of the Two Sicilies to be a traitor. Caracciolo claimed that he was driven by the need to protect his family after the King had fled to Palermo as the French approached Naples.

Discouraging cooperation with the French clearly was important to Britain and her allies in Italy. And Nelson was not acting simply as the British navy commander on the scene; he also had been appointed commander in chief of the Neapolitan navy. To Nelson, Caracciolo was not a vanquished military opponent; he was a traitor and renegade without honor, someone who accepted a military role with the enemy of his country and who was convicted of treason by a Neapolitan jury. The incident was one more example during 1799 of the hard side of Nelson's personality.

~

"Do not think my dear Lord, that my opinion is formed from the arrangements of anyone. No; be it good, or be it bad, it is all my own."

Written from HMS *Foudroyant* to Earl Spencer,
First Lord of the Admiralty, July 1799

When Nelson received a dispatch from his commander in chief, Admiral Lord Keith, that said "you are hereby required and directed to send such Ships as you can possibly spare off the Island of Minorca," he sent none. His rationale was that the safety of the Kingdom of the Two Sicilies was more important than Minorca.

Whether or not he had overstepped his bounds, Nelson was very forthright with his civilian leaders, and he took full responsibility for his actions. It was the type of tough-mindedness that infuriated many of his seniors, including Keith, and made those at the Admiralty and Whitehall exceedingly nervous, including his supporters.

At this particular time, the actions dictated by this mental toughness were thrown into question by the possibility that he was being excessively influenced by Lady Hamilton, whether he recognized it or not.

"I am well aware of the consequences of disobeying my orders; but, as I have often before risked my life for the good Cause, so I with cheerfulness did my commission: for although a Military tribunal may think me criminal, the world will approve my conduct."
Written from Naples to the Duke of Clarence, July 1799

This particular communication with Nelson's friend, the Duke of Clarence, seems suspiciously like an attempt to trump the Admiralty and Whitehall with a royal connection. As it turned out, after Nelson returned to England in 1800, he was conspicuously snubbed at court for his behavior at Palermo and Naples in 1799.

❧

"And I also observe, and with great pain, that their Lordships see no cause which could justify my disobeying the orders of my Commanding Officer, Lord Keith. . . . I have to request that you will have the goodness to assure their Lordships that I knew when I decided on those important points, that perhaps my life, certainly my commission, was at stake by my decision; but, being firmly of opinion that the honour of my King and Country, the dearest object of my heart [were involved], and that to have deserted the cause and person of His Majesty's faithful Ally, His Sicilian Majesty, would have been unworthy my name and their Lordship's former opinion of me, I determined at all risks to support the honour of my gracious Sovereign and Country, and not to shelter myself under the letter of the law, which I shall never do when put in competition with the Public Service."

Written from Palermo to Evan Nepean,
Secretary of the Admiralty, September 1799

Nelson's vigorous defense of his actions at Palermo and Naples in 1799 is concise and unyielding. And, notwithstanding his emotional relationship with Lady Hamilton, his willingness to ignore certain orders during this controversial period of his career was totally consistent with his previous behavior. His determination to act on the basis of the circumstances at hand, rather than orders from afar, was clearly established before 1799. It was shown, for example, in his insistence on enforcing Britain's Navigation Acts in the West Indies during his tour as captain of HMS *Boreas* in 1785, and it was reinforced when he was praised for showing independent initiative at the Battle of Cape St. Vincent in 1797.

❧

"Terror is the only weapon to wield against these people. To talk kindly to them is only to encourage them. Demand nothing that is not just, and never recede, and settle the whole in half-an-hour."

Written from Palermo to Earl Spencer,
First Lord of the Admiralty, November 1799

Nelson's tough-minded approach to diplomatic negotiations was no different for the Muslim leaders of the Mediterranean rim than it was for the small kingdoms in Italy and the Balkans. In describing how he wanted to deal with the Dey of Algiers to the First Lord of the Admiralty, he proposed his usual hardline approach, with a Nelsonian twist that the whole matter should be settled in a half hour.

❧

"I have fought contrary to orders, and I shall perhaps be hanged: never mind, let them."

Attributed by the authors Clarke and M'Arthur to
Nelson at the Battle of Copenhagen, 1 April 1801

At a crucial point in the Battle of Copenhagen, Nelson's commander in chief ordered him to retire. He refused and risked ending his career if defeated. His reaction was one of the noteworthy examples of the mental toughness that matched his physical bravery, and it reflected the battle-hardened personality that made him uniquely successful in combat.

❧

"[F]or if a man consults whether he is to fight, when he has the power in his own hands, it is certain that his opinion is against

*fighting; but that is not the case at present, and I own I do
want good council."*

> Written from HMS *Medusa* at the Downs to
> Henry Addington, Prime Minister, August 1801

At the writing of this letter, Nelson had just been roughly handled by the French in his cross-channel attack on Boulogne. He was advocating a similar attack on Flushing; Earl St. Vincent and Admiral Lord Hood had other ideas. And, although Nelson was weighing the opinions of his seniors, he surely wanted to be certain that it would not be interpreted as a departure from his consistently aggressive doctrine.

～

"[T]ake, sink, burn, and destroy them."

> Written from HMS *Amphion,* off Capri, to Captain Henry
> Richardson, HMS *Juno,* June 1803

When Nelson gave his subordinate officer orders to seek out and attack French troop convoys along the coast of Sardinia, he used a phrase common to the British navy of the time. The order to "take, sink, burn, and destroy" reflected the basically aggressive doctrine of its officers, and was used frequently in orders that were by necessity general. The phrase is a reminder that Nelson's combat aggressiveness had its roots in a deeply embedded preference for the offense in the navy in which he served.

～

*"The French force, yesterday, at two o'clock, was correctly ascertained—eight Sail of the Line, eight Frigates, and five or six
Corvettes, perfectly ready, and as fine as paint can make them.
. . . I only hope in God we shall meet them. Our weather-*

beaten Ships, I have no fears, will make their sides like a
plumb-pudding."
                Written from HMS *Victory,* off Toulon, to Hugh Elliot,
                        British Ambassador at Naples, November 1803

When Nelson wrote to the British Ambassador at Naples about
turning the sides of the French ships into plumb pudding it
reflected a confidence that had basis in reality. During this period,
the French ships spent most of their time in port where they were
well maintained. In contrast, the British navy ships in the
Mediterranean were worked at sea relentlessly. The result was that
the crews under Nelson's command were honed and hardened,
while the French lacked the special toughness that only operational experience can create. These circumstances contributed to
Nelson's conviction that he could defeat the French in combat,
even when he was outnumbered and outgunned.

"I never knew the superior Officers to lead on well but that they
were always bravely supported by the men under their orders.
Wounds must be expected in fighting the Enemy. They are
marks of honour, and our grateful Country is not unmindful
of the sufferings of her gallant defenders. A regular list will be
sent to the Patriotic Fund at Lloyd's, and the Captains are to
give each man a certificate before he leaves the Ship, describing
his wound, signed by the Captain and Surgeon."
                Written from HMS *Victory* to Captain Ross Donnelly,
                                        HMS *Narcissus,* July 1804

In this memorandum, written after a successful boat action in
which Donnelly and *Narcissus* were involved, Nelson emphasized the importance of good planning and courageous leadership. In respect to planning, earlier in the memorandum he

wrote, "without that, bravery would be useless." But the emphasis of his dispatch is on wounds as a visible sign of toughness in battle and the recognition that toughness earned. In some instances there was monetary recognition for wounds not only from the Admiralty but also from groups like Lloyd's of London,[3] whose commercial viability depended on the British navy.

The memorandum reflects the tightly woven social system, combining traditional patriotism with the need to protect national economic interests, that supported the willingness of men like Nelson to risk the dangers of combat.

～

"I am, in truth, half dead; but what man can do to find them out, shall be done; but I must not make more haste than good speed, and leave Sardinia, Sicily, or Naples for them to take, should I go either to the Eastward or Westward, without knowing something more about them."

Written from HMS *Victory* to
Captain Sir Alexander John Ball, April 1805

Nelson's toughness was a major element of his ability to pursue his objective despite fatigue, anxiety, and discouragement. In the months before the Battle of Trafalgar he faced all three of those difficulties to an extreme degree, yet he remained sharply focused on his mission. His ships and crews were overworked; his adversary, French Admiral Villeneuve, was an elusive quarry; and Nelson's military intelligence was meager and frequently faulty. However, Nelson's dogged determination, fused with his exceptional physical endurance and grasp of the strategic factors, was a balancing factor and a force multiplier of immense proportions in battle.

❧

"I went on shore for the first time since the 16th of June 1803; and from having my foot out of the Victory, two years, wanting ten days."

Entry in Nelson's private diary, July 1805

The durability of a naval commander who not only survived, but also maintained effective leadership during two uninterrupted years aboard ship, is astonishing.

❧

"They have done for me at last, Hardy . . . my backbone is shot through . . . my sufferings are great, but they will all be soon over."

Attributed to Nelson by Dr. William Beatty, surgeon aboard HMS *Victory* at the Battle of Trafalgar, 21 October 1805

The French sharpshooter's ball that struck Nelson did indeed sever his spine. For more than three hours he suffered, at times getting reports on the progress of the battle, at times giving orders to his flag captain, Thomas Hardy. Even after hours of suffering, he exhibited his unique combination of physical and mental toughness, along with resignation to his death.

"The acid test of battle brings out the pure metal."
—Gen. George S. Patton, USA

3. Combat

~

"I never saw fear, what is it?"

Attributed to Nelson by one of his grandmothers and
recorded by biographers Clarke and M'Arthur in 1809,
approximately 1763

An apocryphal story told by Nelson's grandmother related an
incident from his early childhood—he could have been about
five years old—that foretold his unusual bravery. The story
described how a search party found him after he had been lost
in a forest area. His grandmother scolded him upon his return
home, observing, "I wonder that fear did not drive you home."
His boyishly brash response about never having seen fear
reflected an attitude that he repeatedly carried into mortal combat in his later life. It also demonstrated, at a very young age, his
instinct for turning a phrase.

"My merit, if that is any, was seizing the happy moment. The Enemy lost many men; we had not a man hurt."
Written from HMS *Agamemnon* to Nelson's brother, the Reverend William Nelson, March 1794

Nelson's description of a commando-like raid to his brother illuminated an important element of his basic combat doctrine: seize the moment. This aspect of Nelson's approach to battle was never more evident or more important than at the later Battle of the Nile on 1 August 1798. After searching the Mediterranean for months, Nelson finally located the French battle fleet at Aboukir Bay.

Although it was towards the end of the day, and night combat at sea was unusual in that era, Nelson attacked without hes-

Nelson's attempt to attack a polar bear using his rifle as a club was an early example of his lack of fear in the face of physical danger. *Nelson's Conflict with a Bear, July 1773;* engraving by J. Landseer from a painting by Richard Westall.

itation. The swiftness of the attack surprised the French and contributed significantly to the overwhelming victory that some believe to be Nelson's most important military achievement. One of the reasons why he was able to attack so quickly was the fact that his captains were thoroughly briefed before action about how Nelson planned to approach the various potential scenarios.

"A brave man runs no more risk than a coward."
Written from HMS *Agamemnon* to his wife, April 1795

Nelson's wife constantly expressed concern for his safety in combat, and went so far as to question the wisdom of his quickness to risk his life. Her concern was understandable, but the ways in which it was expressed also revealed that she didn't understand, or wish to understand, that Nelson's bravery in combat was part of his persona. Nelson tried to get her to appreciate his willingness to risk his personal safety, and his failure in this regard was a principal factor in the erosion of their relationship. In vivid contrast to Fanny's tentative response to her husband's heroics, the British public and Lady Hamilton heaped adulation on him for his astonishing deeds in combat.

"[A] battle without a complete victory is destruction to us, for we cannot get another mast this side of Gibraltar."
Written from HMS *Agamemnon* to Nelson's friend,
Captain William Locker, Lieutenant Governor of
Greenwich Naval Hospital, May 1795

An important combat concept that Nelson helped to establish was that the only satisfactory conclusion for any naval engagement was annihilation of the enemy. Prior to Nelson's time, most sea battles fought by the British navy, even those considered to be victories, ended far short of total destruction of one side or the other. In this instance, Nelson's approach was supported by the specific circumstance that, in May 1795, the British navy could not count on finding naval stores for repairs in the Mediterranean.

∼

"[I]n war much is left to Providence."
Written from HMS *La Minerve* to his wife, January 1797

Among the factors that enabled Nelson to act coolly in battle were his strong religious beliefs. He never feared for his personal safety, assuming that it was in the hands of God. His coolness under fire had a double impact in the chaos of combat. It not only inspired those around him, it allowed him to concentrate on, and take advantage of, the unpredictable events of battle as they unfolded.

∼

"[T]he Admiral made the signal to 'tack in succession;' but I, perceiving the Spanish Ships all to bear up before the wind, or nearly so, evidently with the intention of forming their line going large, joining their separated Division, at that time engaged with some of our centre Ships, or flying from us—to prevent either of their schemes from taking effect, I ordered the ship to be wore."
From *A Few Remarks Relative to Myself,* written and sent to various correspondents soon after the Battle of Cape St. Vincent, February 1797

The courage to risk defeat and disgrace in battle was as much a part of Nelson's character as physical bravery. At a crucial point in the Battle of Cape St. Vincent, he showed brilliant initiative by quickly wearing ship instead of tacking in succession, as initially ordered by his fleet commander, Sir John Jervis. By acting upon Jervis's intent, he precipitated an important British victory. When he broke out of the formation in order to more quickly join the British van and thereby make victory possible, it was the first example of this particular type of bold initiative from him in a major fleet engagement.

His near-fanatical insistence on "doing the right thing" in combat, based on his own judgment of the on-the-scene circumstances, made Nelson unpopular with many in the British navy. In fact, even after the major British victory at Cape St. Vincent, one of his fellow captains, Robert Calder, criticized Nelson's bold action to their commander in chief, then–Admiral Sir John Jervis. Jervis responded to the criticism in a way that surely encouraged Nelson to continue to use his judgment and initiative based on the circumstances of the moment. To Calder's accusation that Nelson had acted beyond his orders, Jervis said: "It certainly was so, and if ever you commit such a breach of your orders, I will forgive you also."

In a later situation with an ironic twist, Calder was to be officially criticized for lack of initiative in an action with the French; Nelson supported him on the basis that it was unfair to make a judgment about the action from afar.

~

"A friend in need is a friend indeed,' was never more truly verified than by your most noble and gallant conduct yesterday in sparing the Captain from further loss."
Written from HMS *Irresistible* to then–Captain Cuthbert
Collingwood, February 1797

Collingwood, in command of HMS *Excellent,* had come to the support of Nelson in HMS *Captain* during the Battle of Cape St. Vincent. And although Nelson was undeniably anxious to enhance his own reputation as a warrior, he also was quick to recognize the valor of his companions in arms, especially those who later came to be known as the Band of Brothers.

Later, at Cape Trafalgar, Vice Admiral Collingwood was to lead the British lee line into battle alongside Nelson's line. At the outset of the conflict Nelson was reported to have remarked, "See how that noble fellow Collingwood carries his ship into action." Collingwood is interred near Nelson, under the great dome of St. Paul's Cathedral.

~

"[I]f our Ships are but carried close by the Officers, I will answer for a British Fleet being always successful."
Written from HMS *Captain* to early Nelson biographer,
John M'Arthur, April 1797

The example of his seniors during his early career, and his combat experiences, taught Nelson that close-in, smashing cannon fire was more effective than the long-range, disabling fire preferred by the French. At the battles of the Nile, Copenhagen, and Trafalgar, driving his ships into extremely close proximity to the enemy for a pell-mell battle was a consistent tactic he employed.

To take advantage of that tactic, Nelson's ships were drilled in rapid-fire, short-range gunnery. Another element of Nelson's combat tactics was the concentration of his own ships against one part of the enemy's force at a time. In the process of focusing his attack this way, Nelson often was able to "double" (attack from both sides) his enemy's ships with devastating effect.

Nelson's tactics were both a result and an accelerator of a change in combat at sea that was taking place during his era. During his time, marked initially by his astonishing victory at the Battle of the Nile, annihilation of the enemy in a battle became a realistic strategic objective.

❧

"The boldest measures are the safest."
Written to Lady Hamilton from Naples, October 1798

The aggressive quality of Nelson's approach to combat was unmistakable. In this letter to Lady Hamilton, written only months after the Battle of the Nile, the success of his extremely bold attack on the French fleet at Aboukir had to be very much in Nelson's mind. The hysterical adulation of the court and populace of the Kingdom of the Two Sicilies, plus mounting fame within Britain, provided reinforcement to the aggressive combat tactics he demonstrated up to that point in his career.

❧

"By attacking the enemy's van and centre, the wind blowing directly along their Line, I was enabled to throw what force I pleased on a few ships."
Written from Palermo to Admiral Lord Howe,
January 1799

Nelson's tactics included doing the unexpected and concentrating his force on selected portions of the enemy fleet. Before the Battle of the Nile, he briefed his captains continuously and thoroughly on his approach to the forthcoming battle. It was a practice considered by many to be part of the legendary Nelson Touch alluded to by him before the Battle of Trafalgar.[1] When the time came to fight, there was no doubt in each captain's mind about his leader's basic combat doctrine.

A corollary to Nelson's combat tactic of concentrating the force of his initial impact on the enemy was the tactic of doubling (attacking from both sides) particular ships of the opposing fleet. This tactic was used with great effect not only at the Battle of the Nile but also at the Battle of Trafalgar.

∿

"[V]ery soon, we must all be content with a plantation of six feet by two, and I probably shall possess this estate much sooner than is generally thought."
Written from Palermo to Vice Admiral Samuel Goodall,
January 1799

Nelson was not physically powerful. He was average in stature and suffered from many physical problems. Among these were his wounds, which had serious lingering effects. Additionally, he suffered a near-fatal tropical fever early in his career, various vague but worrisome heart symptoms, and, perhaps most debilitating, chronic seasickness.

Notwithstanding those physical problems, Nelson exhibited great physical courage in situations that ranged from hand-to-hand combat to the horrific antipersonnel effects of cannon fire directed at a wooden ship. It was as if the emotion of combat overrode all of his bodily weaknesses, and created an inner strength that was clearly perceived by those whom he was leading.

∿

"[I]t is you who taught me to board a Frenchman, by your conduct when in the Experiment; it is you who always told [me], 'Lay a Frenchman close, and you will beat him.'"
Written from Palermo to his friend, Captain William
Locker, Lieutenant Governor of Greenwich
Naval Hospital, February 1799

Nelson served under Captain Locker as a lieutenant aboard HMS *Lowestoffe.* Locker had developed his attitude about naval combat with the French during the Seven Years War, and he passed his opinions about aggressiveness in battle to his junior officers. Although many observers think of Nelson as a tactical innovator, his tactics were based on the influence of captains like Locker and notable British navy admirals who preceded him, like Rodney,

Duncan, Hood, and Jervis. It was actually Nelson's unique ability to apply a winning doctrine to the situation at hand that was so important, rather than the specific tactics he employed.

~

"[V]ictories cannot be obtained without blood."
Written from Palermo to Captain Edward Foote, June 1799

Nelson was not reluctant to pay a price in blood for victory. Despite this attitude, those who fought with him did so without reluctance; in fact, they did so with great emotional commitment to his tactics.

Clearly one of the reasons for the fierce loyalty of those who fought with Nelson was that he risked his own life as willingly as he risked those of others. The evidence was ever visible to those around him from the wounds he suffered at Calvi, the Battle of Santa Cruz, the Battle of the Nile, and elsewhere.

~

"No time should be lost."
Written from Palermo to Chevalier Italinsky, October 1799

An important part of Nelson's fighting doctrine was to initiate combat swiftly. Particularly at the Battle of the Nile, this gave him an initial tactical edge in the ensuing battle.

~

"I don't care a damn by which passage we go, so that we fight them!"
Attributed to Nelson by then–Captain Robert Otway,
HMS *London,* just days before the Battle of
Copenhagen, March 1801

Nelson's impatience when battle was imminent was well known. In this instance he was expressing his frustration with the discussions about the best route to approach the Danish defenses. As Nelson anticipated, the Danes were taking advantage of the delays to strengthen those defenses, and the extreme caution of his commander in chief, Admiral Sir Hyde Parker, made the coming battle situation more difficult. Eventually, Nelson was put in command of a detached squadron for the attack which, thanks to Nelson's negotiations during a cease-fire after victory had been secured, achieved Britain's strategic objectives.

Although he denigrated his own skills in the difficult negotiations, Nelson also was quick to claim that they were instrumental in achieving British strategic objectives. This was one instance when he was able to emerge victorious without totally annihilating the opposition, although there were heavy losses on both sides.

"It is warm work, and this day may be the last to any of us at a moment; but mark you, I would not be elsewhere for thousands."
Attributed to Nelson by then–Colonel The Honorable William Stewart, an eyewitness at the Battle of Copenhagen, 2 April 1801

Under pressure, Nelson had a way of coming up with a memorable phrase. No doubt this helped distract those around him from the potentially lethal action of the moment. It also enhanced his reputation as a fearless combat leader.

"I had their huzzas before—I have their hearts now!"
Attributed by early Nelson biographers, Clarke and M'Arthur, September 1805

When Nelson left Portsmouth for the last time on 14 September, a crowd gathered and cheered him as he and Thomas Hardy, flag captain of HMS *Victory,* pulled away from shore in the admiral's barge. Nelson's comment to Hardy demonstrates that he knew, and appreciated, the difference between the honors given a military hero and the true affection of the public.

The unique and emotional support of the public was one of the important things that strengthened Nelson as he moved towards his final battle and ultimate fame at Trafalgar. He gave the British public the victories over Napoleon they desperately needed, and he drew strength from their visibly emotional response.

"I believe my arrival was most welcome, not only to the Commander of the Fleet, but also to every individual in it."
Written from HMS *Victory* to Lady Hamilton, October 1805

When Nelson arrived shortly before the Battle of Trafalgar to take command of the British fleet, he had the strong support of the captains who would soon be in mortal combat with him. They knew his record as a combat leader and had every confidence in his ability to lead them to success over the French-Spanish Combined Fleet. That confidence was in sharp contrast to the morale in the French and Spanish fleets, and was an important plus for the British navy when the fighting began.

"[I]t is . . . annihilation that the Country wants, and not merely a splendid Victory . . . honourable to the parties concerned, but absolutely useless in the extended scale to bring Buonaparte to his marrow-bones."
Written from HMS *Victory* to The Right Honorable
George Rose, Nelson's friend and confidant of
Prime Minister Pitt, October 1805

There can be no doubt that Nelson was committed to total victory over the French-Spanish Combined Fleet at Trafalgar. His commitment to annihilating the enemy in combat was clearly demonstrated at the Battle of the Nile, and strikingly repeated at Trafalgar.

Nelson's recognition of the necessity for total victory was one of the ways he demonstrated that he was not just a brilliant naval tactician. He also had an understanding of the strategic potential of naval power that predated the theories of Mahan and other sea power advocates who were to follow.[2]

∼

"But, in case Signals can neither be seen or perfectly understood, no Captain can do very wrong if he places his Ship alongside that of an Enemy."
> Written from HMS *Victory* to Nelson's captains before the Battle of Trafalgar, October 1805

Nelson's memorandum before the Battle of Trafalgar included detailed instructions for his captains. It also included, in a single sentence, one of the best combat doctrines ever provided to a force heading into combat. And it was Nelson's doctrine, more than the strategy of Britain's leaders or his own tactics, that made Nelson a naval combat leader unsurpassed in history.

∼

"Engage the enemy more closely."
> Last signal made before combat was joined at the Battle of Trafalgar, 21 October 1805

At the beginning of the battles of the Nile and Copenhagen, Nelson had made the same signal. It provided a shorthand message to his fleet that summed up his combat doctrine.

∼

"[M]ay humanity after victory be the predominant feature in the British fleet."
> From Nelson's last diary, written just before the Battle of Trafalgar, October 1805

Although Nelson was fierce in battle, he had, in general, a genuine regard for his adversaries. He shared a quality exhibited by many combat leaders, a humane concern for those, friend and foe, caught up in the horrors of combat.

It is worth noting that, on at least one occasion, Nelson himself was the beneficiary of this combatants' code. After the resounding defeat of the amphibious assault he led against the Spanish at Santa Cruz in the Canary Islands in 1797, the commander of the Spanish force, General Antonio Gutiérrez, showed great humanity towards Nelson and the defeated British force.

∽

"They have done for me at last, Hardy . . . my backbone is shot through."
Attributed to Nelson by Dr. William Beatty, surgeon aboard
HMS *Victory* at the Battle of Trafalgar, 21 October 1805

At Trafalgar, Nelson paid the ultimate price in combat. His words at the moment of his lethal wound, as those in earlier circumstances, strongly suggest he anticipated that death was imminent. For example, in October of 1803, he wrote to Lady Hamilton, "[S]ome ball may soon close all my accounts with this world of care and vexation!"

Even under the stress of the situation he was calm and behaved in accordance with what he had preached during his career: death comes to all, and those who go into combat must be prepared for it. In a different context five years before Trafalgar, he had cited a homespun phrase that summed up his fatalism: "[T]he pitcher never goes often to the well, but it comes home broke at last."

Nelson came "home broke at last" on the quarterdeck of *Victory*. The spot where the musket ball felled him is marked with a small but evocative brass plaque that reads, "Here Nelson Fell—21st October 1805."

"The Royal Navy can claim a singular position in history."
—Rear Admiral J. R. Hill, RN (Ret.)

4. Nelson's Navy

"The perseverance of our Fleet has been great, and to that only can be attributed our unexampled success. . . . I believe the world is convinced that no conquests of importance can be made without us; and yet, as soon as we have accomplished the service we are ordered upon, we are neglected . . . all we get is honour and salt beef."

Written from HMS *Agamemnon* at Naples to his wife, September 1793

Nelson's fierce pride in the professional performance of the British navy was accompanied by a belief that its important achievements were not appreciated by Britain's deskbound political leadership of the time. Notwithstanding Nelson's complaint, there was little bitterness in this letter to Fanny. It was, in fact, a newsy and matter-of-fact recounting of such varied events as the occupation of Toulon by the British and the possibility of some prize money from the capture of a ship from Smyrna.

The letter closed with a postscript about being becalmed in Naples Bay with an impressive view of Mount Vesuvius. Nelson had been sent to Naples to secure military support from the Kingdom of the Two Sicilies for the occupation of Toulon. There, his first meeting with Sir William and Lady Hamilton was imminent, and his view of Mount Vesuvius portended anything but calm for his marriage.

∾

"My Ship's company behaved most amazingly well. They begin to look upon themselves as invincible, almost invulnerable: believe they would fight a good battle with any Ship of two decks out of France."

Entry in Nelson's journal while aboard HMS *Agamemnon,* off Bastia, March 1794

At the time of this journal entry, Nelson was in command of *Agamemnon,* a 64-gun ship that was among the smaller ships of the line. The *Agamemnon* was exceptionally fast and well-found, and Nelson anticipated an active tour. Many crew members were recruited from the Norfolk region where Nelson grew up, and many in the crew had served with him in his former ships, adding an additional reason for his confidence in his crew. It is generally believed that *Agamemnon* was Nelson's favorite ship.

∾

"His Lordship wished to attack them; a Council of Flag–officers prevented him."

Written from a British army camp near Calvi, Corsica, to his wife, June 1794

Nelson usually did not look upon war councils with favor; he believed they often were a cause of indecisive leadership. The council referred to in this letter consisted of an unusually large

From the decks of these ships, Nelson and his captains changed the course of history. Portraits of HMS *Agamemnon, Captain, Vanguard, Elephant,* and *Victory*; engraving by J. Fittler, from a painting by Nicholas Pocock.

number of flag officers—eight—for a squadron of thirteen ships of the line.

On the positive side of the Calvi operation, however, and despite the serious wound to his right eye suffered there, the action was an example of Nelson working effectively with the British army.

"This day twelve months, my dear Fanny, our Troops landed here to attempt the conquest of the Island, at least of those parts which the French were in possession of; and, however lightly the acquisition of Corsica may be deemed by many in England, yet I take upon me to say it was a measure founded on great wisdom; and during the war must be ever of the most essential service to us, and very detrimental to our Enemies. . . . So much

*for the value of Corsica—I have done; the recollection of one
short year brings it to my mind. It was Lord Hood's plan, and
it was accomplished chiefly by seamen."*

Written from St. Fiorenzo, Corsica, to his wife,
February 1795

These lines were part of a letter to Fanny expounding the strategic importance of Corsica to Britain. The full letter reads like a
briefing for young naval officers enrolled in a course on geopolitical strategy. It is particularly interesting in that it suggests that
Nelson believed that Fanny was intelligent enough to comprehend "male" subjects related to his profession. It also is a reminder
that Nelson had a unique grasp of the broader implications of the
naval actions in which he was involved.

∼

"Nothing can stop the courage of English seamen."
Written from St. Fiorenzo, Corsica, to his wife, April 1795

An important part of Nelson's supreme self-confidence was his
deep conviction that the British navy's seamen were unmatched
in skill and courage. That conviction was apparent to those in
the lower decks, and they responded by living up to his expectations in the performance of their duty. One of the interesting sidelights of the courage of the British seamen of the time
was their tradition of entering battle with vociferous cheering.
This custom was not without its psychological effect on the
enemy.

∼

*"We are put to sea, not only as being more honourable, but also
as much safer, than skulking in Port . . . our zeal does not in the
least justify the gross neglect of the new Admiralty Board. . . .
Had not our late action proved more distressing to the Enemy*

than the Admiralty had any right to suppose, we should before
this time have been driven out of the Mediterranean."
Written from HMS *Agamemnon* to his uncle
William Suckling, April 1795

By 1795 Nelson was an experienced, combat-hardened officer. He, like many naval officers in a similar position, believed that the rear echelon political and naval leaders neither understood local circumstances nor appreciated the performance of the people who had to deal with on-scene circumstances. On the same day he wrote this letter to his uncle, Nelson wrote to his father sharply complaining about how badly the Admiralty was managing matters in the Mediterranean.

The main problem from the point of view of Nelson and his commander in chief, Vice Admiral William Hotham, was that the Admiralty and Whitehall were not providing a sufficient number of ships to deal with the French naval threat in the Mediterranean.

The reference to "our late action" presumably is an allusion to a brush between a force led by Hotham and a French force on 13 and 14 March. During the action on 13 March, Nelson led a skillful attack by his ship, *Agamemnon,* on the French *Ça Ira,* considerably larger than *Agamemnon.* Nelson's attack contributed to the capture of the *Ça Ira,* plus another ship, the next day.

Nelson complained in a later letter to his wife that Hotham should have been more aggressive when provided with an opportunity for a major action with the French. Instead, Hotham broke off the action saying: "We must be contented, we have done very well." Nelson's comment to Fanny was one of the many statements illuminating his warrior's attitude, which was to have strong influence on many generations of British naval officers. He wrote, "Sure I am, had I commanded our Fleet of the 14th, that either the whole French Fleet would have graced my triumph, or I should have been in a confounded scrape." The comment also showed that—at least in Nelson's opinion—not all of his flag officer seniors had a sufficiently aggressive approach to dealing with the French at sea.

⌇

"Here we have been exactly one week, and can hear no accounts from England, nor have we for upwards of three weeks past. It is extraordinary that neither messenger nor post should arrive; but the great folks at home forget us at a distance."
Written from Leghorn to his uncle William Suckling,
May 1795

One of the greatest problems Nelson and his fellow officers contended with in the Mediterranean was slowness of communications. Although his complaint about the neglect of "the great folks at home" may have at times been justified, the slowness and unreliability of communications was a common problem for all naval commanders of his era. Ships carrying dispatches were subject to weather problems and interception by the enemy. Even when dispatches and letters arrived in an area, connecting with a ship that operated without precise predictability compounded the problem. The lack of fast communications and the corollary lack of reliable intelligence were among the most serious and consistent challenges that Nelson overcame with his dogged persistence and sound strategic instincts.

⌇

"Oh, miserable Board of Admiralty! They have forced the first Officer in our Service away from his command."
Written from HMS *Agamemnon* to his brother,
the Reverend William Nelson, June 1795

Lord Hood was a fighting admiral and a senior officer who had advanced Nelson's career on more than one occasion. In April of 1795, Hood wrote a blunt letter to the Admiralty pointing out the problems among the British ships in the Mediterranean caused by the Admiralty's failure to provide proper support to its deployed forces. As a reward for his honesty, the Admiralty relieved Hood of his command as he was about to return to the Mediterranean as the commander in chief in that area. The shabby treatment of Hood certainly contributed to Nelson's qualified opinion of the Admiralty.

"Far be it from me to detract from Admiral Hotham's merits, for a better heart no man possesses, and he is ever kind and attentive to me; but between the abilities of him and Lord Hood can be no comparison."

Written from HMS *Agamemnon* to his friend, Captain William Locker, Lieutenant Governor of Greenwich Naval Hospital, August 1795

Nelson's chief criterion for judging his naval superiors was not necessarily their treatment of him—both Hotham and Hood praised Nelson's performance of duty—but the degree of aggressiveness in their leadership. Twelve days after this letter, he wrote to his friend, then–Captain Cuthbert Collingwood, and was more pointed in his criticism of Hotham. He wrote: "Our Admiral, *entre nous,* has no political courage whatever, and is alarmed at the mention of any strong measure."

"I here beg leave to mention a circumstance which I dare say you hear of in the Fleet—the badness of the lemons. . . . I know, Sir, you must be interested in whatever concerns the health of the Seamen, which is my reason for mentioning this circumstance."

Written from HMS *Agamemnon* to Admiral Sir John Jervis, May 1796

The health of the crews in Nelson's ships was a primary concern for him. He understood that a disease like scurvy could seriously reduce the fighting capability of his ships, and he paid a great deal of attention to the availability of citrus fruit and fresh vegetables for his crews. This vigorous attention to the physical well-being of the sailors on whom he relied in combat was one element in the combination of factors that added up to his crucial victories.

"Indeed, the French say, they are Masters on shore, and the English at sea."
                    Written from HMS *Captain* to his wife, June 1796

This comment accurately summarized the military strategies of Britain and France during the Napoleonic Wars. For the British, their primary military instrument of foreign policy was the British navy; for Napoleon, it was his army. Britain's heavy reliance on her navy at this historical juncture was one of the reasons why Nelson became a national hero of such huge proportions.

"I suppose England will be the last to make peace; and whilst she trusts to her Wooden Walls, she [will] be more successful than any other Power. This has ever been proved, yet we continue blindly to be attached to the Army."
                    Written from HMS *Captain* to Nelson's brother,
                    the Reverend William Nelson, June 1796

As it turned out, it was indeed the "Wooden Walls" of the British navy that turned the tide against Napoleon. However, from Nelson's perspective the importance of the role played by the British navy in comparison to that of the British army was never properly recognized.

~

"I had the happiness to command a Band of Brothers; therefore, night was to my advantage. Each knew his duty, and I was sure each would feel for a French ship."
Written from Palermo to Admiral of the Fleet
Earl Howe, January 1799

Nelson frequently referred to the captains who served under him as his Band of Brothers. Some, like Troubridge and Collingwood, were friends of many years standing. All were highly professional naval officers who were imbued with an exceptional loyalty to Nelson and a fighting spirit that mirrored his own.

This particular reference to his Band of Brothers was an allusion to the Battle of the Nile. At the beginning of that battle, Captain Thomas Foley, whose ship HMS *Goliath* led the British battle line, took his ship around the van of the French line and down the landward side of the enemy ships. Because of the proximity of shoal water and lack of Admiralty charts, it was a risky maneuver. However, Foley's use of his seaman's instincts and his determination to attack at close quarters snatched the initiative for Nelson's force. It was exactly the kind of combat behavior that endeared the Band of Brothers to Nelson.

~

"You will always keep in mind how much the service requires active, not passive service."
Written from HMS *Vanguard* in Palermo to Captain Darby,
HMS *Bellerophon*, March 1799

After fairly lengthy orders concerning detached convoy duty, which began with the traditional "you are hereby required and directed," Nelson ends his dispatch to Captain Darby with this interesting admonition about the general requirement for active service by the British navy's ships. The principle that attention to duty required a proactive attitude was a companion to Nelson's aggressive combat doctrine.

It is an interesting historical side note that, at the time he was reminding Captain Darby of the need for active service, Nelson was going through a period during which he was widely criticized. During the year 1799 he refused to abandon his close attention to the Kingdom of the Two Sicilies in Palermo and Naples, and coincidentally his proximity to Lady Hamilton.

"Our Ships are very healthy, and I have no doubt, from the constant attention of our Captains, will always be kept so."
Written from Palermo to Admiral Earl St. Vincent,
May 1799

Nelson recognized that there was a close correlation between the health of his seamen and the performance of their duty. And he understood the importance of maintaining a diet that would avoid scurvy, one of the principal health problems for seamen of the era. He also believed that constant activity was a positive factor in their health and morale.

"We have a report that you are going home. This distresses us most exceedingly, and myself in particular. . . . We look up to you, as we have always found you, as to our Father, under whose fostering care we have been led to fame. If, my dear Lord, I have any weight in your friendship, let me entreat you to arouse the sleeping lion. Give not up a particle of your authority to any one; be again our St. Vincent, and we shall be happy."
Written from Palermo to Admiral Earl St. Vincent,
June 1799

Earl St. Vincent was one of Nelson's strongest supporters at the most senior levels of the British navy. As Admiral Sir John

Jervis, he had greatly benefited from Nelson's risky initiative while commanding HMS *Captain* at the Battle of Cape St. Vincent. And, in fact, it was that battle that had earned Jervis his earldom. Despite a later difference over prize money, the relationship of patron and protégé endured. Nelson's plea for St. Vincent to remain as commander in chief of the Mediterranean Fleet surely was based on loyalty and high regard for his mentor. He probably also sensed that St. Vincent's relief might not be so compatible; he was right. As it turned out, Vice Admiral Lord Keith, who took over St. Vincent's Mediterranean command, and Nelson did not get along well.

"I had the full tide of honour, but little real comfort. If the War goes on, I shall be knocked off by a ball, or killed with chagrin. My conduct is measured by the Admiralty, by the narrow rule of law, when I think it should have been done by that of common sense. I restored a faithful Ally by breach of orders, Lord Keith lost a Fleet by obedience, against his own sense. Yet as one is censured, the other must be approved. Such things are."
Written from Palermo to his friend and agent,
Alexander Davison, September 1799

These brutally blunt lines written to his friend sharply focus on one reason why Nelson was not universally popular at the Admiralty. He frequently was simultaneously self-righteous and right. Whether or not he was influenced in his decisions at this time by Lady Hamilton, Nelson was instrumental in saving arguably the most important of Britain's Mediterranean allies in its struggle with Napoleon. However, his ignoring of orders that he believed to be in conflict with his overriding mission was consistent with his past actions. His final statement, "Such things are," reflects a degree of acceptance of the price for his kind of leadership.

∼

"I own I do not believe the Brest fleet will return to sea; and if they do, the Lord have mercy on them, for our Fleet will not, I am sure."

> Written from HMS *Foudroyant* at Leghorn to
> Vice Admiral Lord Keith, June 1800

This comment, thrown out in a petulant letter to his commander in chief, reflects not only Nelson's confidence in the abilities and aggressiveness of his fleet in the Mediterranean but the combat capability of the British navy in general.

∼

"I have not the smallest interest at the Admiralty."

> Written from Merton to Captain Sir Edward Berry,
> February 1802

Many aspects of the British navy of Nelson's time were built on influence, referred to as "interest," and he took his obligation to help relatives of friends and fellow officers very seriously. However, despite his successes in battle and heroic standing with the public, Nelson frequently complained that his victories never translated into interest at the Admiralty. In fact, three days after his letter to Captain Berry, he voiced the same complaint in a letter to Captain Samuel Sutton, HMS *Amazon*. To some extent Nelson's lack of political leverage at the Admiralty was probably due to his frequently abrasive relationship with that institution. Also, this letter was written during a brief period of peace between Britain and France, a time when the opportunities for naval officers were limited.

One of the most difficult situations in regard to leverage at the Admiralty occurred after the Battle of Copenhagen in April of 1801. Nelson's commander in chief at the battle, Admiral Sir Hyde Parker, was notorious for his favoritism. After the battle Hyde Parker secured the promotions of many who were present at the scene but who did not actually participate in the combat. And, in the process, Hyde Parker ignored others who distinguished themselves in the fighting. Nelson sought to redress the injustice with limited success, and the aftermath of that battle was a source of ongoing bitterness for him.

≈

"Their Lordships may rely on my strict obedience to their orders, and I rely with confidence on their liberal constructions of my actions."
Written from HMS *Victory* to Sir Evan Nepean,
Secretary of the Admiralty, May 1803

It is doubtful that the above response to orders concerning Nelson's assignment as commander in chief in the Mediterranean created a sense of calm at the Admiralty.

≈

"Our Master-Ropemaker is a child of thirteen years of age, and the best Ropemaker in the Fleet."
Written from HMS *Victory* at Madalena Islands to Nathaniel
Taylor, naval storekeeper at Malta, November 1803

During the Age of Sail, children were an integral part of the crews of British navy ships. Nelson himself went to sea as a midshipman at the age of twelve.

≈

"I am distressed for Frigates, which are the eyes of the Fleet."
Written from HMS *Victory* to Gen. Sir John Acton,
de facto prime minister at the Court of
Their Sicilian Majesties, January 1804

Nelson frequently was troubled by a lack of frigates at crucial points in his career. Never was this lack felt more keenly than during the many stressful months he spent hunting for the French Toulon Fleet before the Battle of Trafalgar.

"Although my career is nearly run, yet it would embitter my future days and expiring moments, to hear our Navy being sacrificed to the Army."

Written from HMS *Victory* to Captain Sir
Thomas Troubridge, May 1804

The British navy and the British army were not immune to interservice squabbles. At this point, a dispute had arisen over army artillery officers who were assigned to naval bomb vessels and who had refused to allow the soldiers under their command to be assigned duties by the captains of their ships. For Nelson, this struck at the heart of the absolute authority of the captain of a ship. He also feared that if the army "once gain the step of being independent of the Navy on board a Ship . . . they will soon have the other, and command us."

"In Sea affairs, nothing is impossible, and nothing improbable."

Written from HMS *Victory* to Count Mocenigo at Corfu,
August 1804

This statement was part of a letter to the Count that spoke to the possibility that a French fleet under Admiral La Touche-Tréville might be able to continue to evade Nelson. It reflects Nelson's supreme confidence in the capabilities of the ships under his command and the British navy in general. In a different letter written on the same date Nelson wrote, "I command, for Captains and Crews, such a Fleet, as I never have before seen; and it is impossible that any Admiral can be happier situated."

❧

"I am in total ignorance of the intentions of the Admiralty, and I find that the Frigates are ordered from aloft to join you, and at a moment when I have fancied that at least double the number are wanted; but the orders of the Admiralty must be obeyed. I only hope Officers will not be blamed for the events which it is not difficult to foresee will happen."

Written from HMS *Victory* to Vice Admiral
Cuthbert Collingwood, July 1805

The heart of the problem in this situation was one that haunted Nelson in the Mediterranean, a shortage of frigates. His reference to officers being blamed for the consequences of decisions made "from aloft" was a realistic concern for him and for many senior naval officers before and since his time.

❧

"[W]hen their Lordships take into account that the poor Sailor who claims his due, has been for these last two years shut up from every comfort of the shore, and in want of his little pittance . . . I am sure they will agree with me in the propriety of its being immediately paid."

Written from HMS *Victory* to William Marsden,
First Secretary to the Admiralty, August 1805

Prize money was not a factor only for admirals, captains, and officers. The shares for the individual crew members, although relatively small, were very important to those men. Nelson's letter to the Admiralty was only one of many instances of his standing up for the seamen who served Britain so well.

"Nothing can be finer than the Fleet under my command."
Written from HMS *Victory* to Alexander Davison,
September 1805

When all was said and done, Nelson's intense pride in his navy was based not only on its leadership, as significant as that was, but on powerful traditions that had developed over generations.

"Captains are to look to their particular Line as their rallying point. But, in case Signals can neither be seen or perfectly understood, no Captain can do very wrong if he places his Ship alongside that of an Enemy."
Written from HMS *Victory* off Cadiz to his captains
and admirals, October 1805

This statement of a combat doctrine was part of detailed memorandum intended to establish the tactics to be used against the French-Spanish Combined Fleet at the Battle of Trafalgar; it is one of the best statements of a combat doctrine recorded in naval annals. It also is noteworthy as an expression of Nelson's confidence in the admirals and ship captains in his fleet. This combination of a clear combat doctrine and subordinates who could be relied upon to seize initiative as circumstances dictated during battle was an essential piece of Nelson's history-making naval victories. They also became important elements in the naval traditions that led to Britain's dominance of the seas for the century that followed Nelson's victory at Cape Trafalgar on 21 October 1805.

> "Politics is the science of how who gets
> what, when and why."
> —Sidney Hillman

5. Politics

≈

*"I have paid my visit to Lord Howe, who asked me if I wished
to be employed, which I told him I did, therefore it is likely he
will give me a Ship."*

Written from London to Nelson's friend,
Captain William Locker, January 1784

Once a British navy officer reached the rank of post captain,
advancement in rank was driven by the retirement and death
of those above him on the seniority list. Getting command of a
good ship was another matter. That process was a subtle blend
of seniority, combat performance, connections, and luck. The
process was also a special, singularly naval brand of the British
politics of the era.

Much of the lobbying for a command was done at what is
now known as the Old Admiralty in London.[1] There, a captain
could wait for days for an opportunity to plead his case for a
good command. And, in a historical side note, it was while

waiting in one of the anterooms of another official building, the
Colonial Office in Downing Street, that the two principal military authors of Napoleon's defeat, Nelson and Wellington, met
for the first and only time.

❧

*"[T]here is nothing like kicking down the ladder a man rises
by."*
Written from the British encampment at Bastia, Corsica,
to Admiral Lord Hood, July 1794

This observation was a postscript at the end of a letter to Nelson's commander in chief; it dealt with what appeared to be
petty political army-navy antagonisms. In fact, in the last line of
the letter, which dealt largely with what Nelson did or did not
say to his army counterparts, he asks Hood to burn the letter,
presumably to prevent it from ever falling into the hands of the
army! The reference to kicking down the ladder a man rises by
is a rather blunt reference to eliminating a potentially troublesome army aide-de-camp by neutralizing his boss. And it was
evidence of the kind of very rough interservice politics that
remains a constant among military services in general.

❧

*"I have just received a letter from the Viceroy of Corsica, in
which are the following flattering expressions to me . . . 'I know
that you, who have had such an honourable share in this acquisition, will not be indifferent at the prosperity of the Country
which you have so much assisted to place under his Majesty's
government'—Whether these are words of course, and to be
forgotten, I know not; they are pleasant, however, for the time."*
Written from San Fiorenzo, Corsica, to his wife,
November 1794

Even at this point before he became a national hero of unique dimensions, Nelson understood that praise from politicians did not necessarily have a tangible payoff for a career naval officer. In future years, he would have numerous opportunities to become even more cynical about the words of politicians.

~

"[A] Minister may be continued too long at a particular Court; he thus becomes imperceptibly the friend of that Court, when he ought to be the jealous observer of their conduct."
Written from HMS *Agamemnon* to Admiral Sir John Jervis, May 1796

Because of Jervis's inclination to send Nelson on detached assignments, Nelson had ample opportunity to observe British ministers in the variety of kingdoms bordering the northern shore of the central Mediterranean. This gratuitous opinion to his senior officer, offered "between ourselves," indicates that he had a close working relationship on matters political as well as military with his commander in chief and mentor.

~

"Almighty God has made me the happy instrument in destroying the Enemy's Fleet, which I hope will be a blessing to Europe."
Written from HMS *Vanguard* to Sir William Hamilton, August 1798

The British defeat of the French battle fleet at the Battle of the Nile was a strategically momentous event, and Nelson saw it in that broad context. His ability to grasp not only the tactical factors of a battle, but the geopolitically strategic implications as well, was a hallmark of his career. That understanding also was a prelude to the sea power concepts that would be articulated later in the nineteenth century by navalists such as Britain's Julian Corbett and America's Alfred Thayer Mahan.

❧

"[A] Government that only exists by the caprice of a mob cannot last."

Written from Palermo to Admiral Earl St. Vincent,
January 1799

In this letter Nelson was speaking of Naples. He had a deeply rooted fear of the gruesome political chaos that invariably followed the overthrow of almost any monarchy. And the shocking excesses of revolutionary France's republican governments were the main source of that feeling.

❧

"[A]lthough we might at one day hope to be at peace with France, we must ever be at war with French principles."

Attributed to Nelson from remarks he made at a ceremony
in Exeter, honoring him for his victory at the
Battle of the Nile, January 1801

Nelson associated the excesses of the French Revolution with antireligious republicanism, which he saw as an international political scourge. He also was strongly influenced by his belief that France was attempting to deny Britain's rightful influence on the politics of Europe. As a result, he deeply felt that French hegemony in Europe had to be prevented at all costs.

❧

"All I have gathered of our first plans, I disapprove most exceedingly; honour may arise from them, good cannot."

Written from HMS *St. George* to Nelson's friend,
Alexander Davison, March 1801

Nelson was confronted with a difficult situation as the British fleet under the command of Admiral Sir Hyde Parker prepared for its mission in the Baltic against Denmark and the League of

Armed Neutrality. Hyde Parker had not maintained his earlier combat reputation in the later years of his career, and Nelson, as second in command, had little confidence in him. In addition, he was frustrated by Hyde Parker's reluctance to get his fleet underway for the Baltic. Nelson correctly believed that continued delay would give the Danes additional time to prepare their defenses.

Somewhat out of character, Nelson used patient political maneuvering with his friend then–Captain Thomas Troubridge, at the time a Lord Commissioner at the Admiralty, and his mentor Earl St. Vincent, then–First Lord of the Admiralty, to address the problem. As a result of his political, nonconfrontational approach, the fleet eventually departed on its mission and, in the end, Nelson was eventually able to establish his influence on the conduct of the mission.

Nelson continued to avoid an open conflict with Hyde Parker as the fleet made its way towards Copenhagen, but along the way he was successful in convincing his commander in chief to allow him to command a detached force to attack the Danes at Copenhagen. The result was a hard-fought victory of long-range strategic importance to Britain.

"[T]he moment of a complete victory was surely the proper time to make an opening with the Nation we had been fighting with."

Written from HMS *St. George* to Henry Addington,
Prime Minister, May 1801

In this letter to his penultimate political leader, the prime minister, Nelson explained why he ended the Battle of Copenhagen at the moment when he had achieved a victory over the Danes. It was an approach that contrasted dramatically with his victories of annihilation over the French at the Battle of the Nile and later over the French and Spanish at the Battle of Trafalgar.

Notwithstanding his protestations from time to time that he was a plain seaman who lacked political skills, by ending the battle with the Danes before the point of their utter destruction, and by taking a major part in the resulting negotiations, he achieved a double objective. He accomplished the military victory Britain sought plus a geopolitical victory on a grand scale, one that avoided perpetuating Denmark as a long-term enemy of the British in the Baltic.

"[T]he moment the Enemy touch our Coast . . . they are to be attacked by every man afloat and on shore: this must be perfectly understood. Never fear the event."

Part of a memorandum by Nelson on defense against an anticipated French invasion of Britain, July 1801

After his success at the Battle of Copenhagen, Nelson was put in command of the British anti-invasion forces in the Channel, including the volunteer Sea Fencibles. Towards the end of a detailed description of the resources and tactics to be used in the event of a French invasion, Nelson set forth that the volunteers must be imbued with the same aggressive doctrine established throughout the regular British navy forces. He was addressing the same requirement that exists today in maintaining any nation's naval reserve force as a viable component of its naval power. And it was another example of Nelson establishing a doctrine that was intended to be the foundation for combat tactics. However, in this circumstance, the combat situation did not materialize.

"I am used and abused; and so far from making money, I am spending the little I have. . . . I am aware none of the Ministry care for me, beyond what suits themselves."

Written to Nelson's friend, Alexander Davison, probably from Deal, England, August 1801

Shortly before this letter was written, Nelson had been in command during an unsuccessful attack on the French invasion forces in Boulogne. That defeat and other, personal matters had to have weighed heavily on him. His accumulated frustration with his political leadership was, under the circumstances, very close to the surface.

⤴

"I have not only wrote it, but impressed it on Mr. Addington's mind, the necessity of his steering such a course as would neither throw the Mamelukes or Turks into the arms of France. Whether they attend at home to these things, I very much doubt and deplore."

Written from HMS *Victory* to Sir Alexander Ball,
Governor of Malta, October 1803

Building and maintaining politico-military alliances were critical parts of the British strategy for containing Napoleon. As with other situations, Nelson was able to see the broad strategic picture in the Mediterranean in 1803. Also as with other situations, he showed how little confidence he had that his political leaders would pay much attention to the input provided by an on-scene senior naval officer.

⤴

"You are right to be as quiet as you can, although it is vexing to be unemployed at such a moment; but it is useless to fret oneself to death, when the folks aloft don't care a pin about it."

Written from HMS *Victory* to
Captain Sir Edward Berry, October 1803

Berry was one of Nelson's Band of Brothers and an officer distinguished in combat. A few years after this exchange of letters, Berry commanded HMS *Agamemnon,* purported to be Nelson's favorite ship, at the Battle of Trafalgar. However, Nelson's letter indicates that Berry was without a command in October 1803, and securing a prestigious and promising command in the British navy of the time was as much a matter of politics as past professional performance. There simply were not enough major ships to go around for the navy's high-quality captains. Nelson's advice to his colleague reflected his low opinion of the Admiralty and Whitehall seniors who entered into such decisions.

"Government don't care much for us."
Written from HMS *Victory* to Lady Hamilton, July 1804

This comment jumps out at the end of a relatively long letter that included references to his poor health and lack of prize money, and it reflected both fatigue and political cynicism. For Nelson, his overseas assignments, combined with the slowness of communication with his naval and political leaders, often led to a feeling that neither the Admiralty nor Whitehall understood or was concerned about his circumstances. That feeling no doubt contributed to Nelson's frequently expressed opinion that he was justified in modifying orders that came from deskbound administrators in London.

"We made use of the Peace, not to recruit our Navy, but to be the cause of its ruin."
Written from HMS *Victory* to Hugh Elliot,
British Ambassador at Naples, July 1804

In March of 1802 Britain signed the Treaty of Amiens with France.[2] The British government, led by Prime Minister Henry Addington, saw the Treaty as a pause to regroup in its ongoing struggle against France. And many in Britain saw the Treaty as grossly unfavorable to their country. Addington had appointed Earl St. Vincent as First Lord of the Admiralty and, although the British navy's ship numbers were maintained at a level of marginal superiority during the period, St. Vincent created turmoil among the private shipyards with his efforts at financial reforms. Although Nelson had great personal loyalty towards St. Vincent, he also understood that dissipating one's naval strength, including its industrial infrastructure, would eventually be paid for with British blood.

In the spring of 1803 the British declared war on France once again. As the commander in the Mediterranean, Nelson occupied one of the most strategically pivotal points, that where government policies meet military realities. From his perspective, the pause in the conflict with France between the spring of 1802 and the renewal of hostilities in the spring of 1803 was a missed opportunity to increase the navy's marginal edge over the French at sea. In his comments to Hugh Elliot, Nelson was focused on the kind of politico-military problem that to this day is faced by nations that rely on sea power to protect their national interests.

"Admiral Gantheaume, I see, has hoisted his Flag at Brest; a sure indication to my mind, that at least a part of that Fleet is destined for the Mediterranean. . . . I trust our Government will take care not to allow a superiority, beyond my power of resistance, to get into the Mediterranean."

Written from HMS *Victory* to General Sir John Acton, de facto prime minister to the King of the Kingdom of the Two Sicilies, July 1804

Nelson understood the complexity of Britain's "blue water" geopolitical strategy, and he was aware that factors beyond his immediate theater were connected to his own fate as commander in chief in the Mediterranean. He knew it was up to Whitehall to maintain a British naval force in the Mediterranean that could cope with whatever naval force the French deployed to the theater. Nelson clearly was uneasy about having his and his fleet's fate determined by political decisions made in London.

∽

"I am not one of those who think, that the safety of the State depends on any one, or upon one hundred men; let them go off the stage, and others would ably supply their places."
Written from HMS *Victory* to Major General Villettes,
about July 1804

A monarchist, Nelson also strongly believed in Britain's parliamentary form of political representation.

∽

"Sir John Orde was sent, if it was a Spanish War, to take the money . . . and now he is to wallow in wealth, whilst I am left a beggar. But such things are. I receive the kindest letters from Lord Melville and the Secretary of State, but they think the French Fleet is prize enough for me."
Written from HMS *Victory* to Hugh Elliot,
British Ambassador at Naples, January 1805

Prize money was an important economic issue for British navy officers. Many amassed huge fortunes from their captures at sea. Nelson's brilliant combat career yielded only modest financial returns from this practice. And, at times, he showed bitterness towards any politics at the Admiralty and Whitehall that influenced the assignment of officers to commands with a high potential for prize money. Admiral Sir John Orde was among those senior admirals who amassed fortunes from prize money while not overly distinguishing themselves in combat. He also was among those who resented the official tolerance of Nelson's independent aggressiveness.

In fact Nelson was, to a significant extent, a victim of his own

Notwithstanding Admiralty and Whitehall politics, Nelson was in command at the Battle of Trafalgar, where he achieved a victory of great political importance to Britain. *Close of the Battle of Trafalgar, October 21, 1805*; engraving by J. Fittler, from a painting by Nicholas Pocock.

attitude and reputation for achieving victory in combat. Instead of getting assignments that provided opportunities for wealth, he was given assignments of great strategic importance to Britain. Nelson often boasted that it was honor and glory in battle that motivated him, not prize money. However, his frustration at being taken at his word showed through from time to time.

"It is, as Mr. Pitt knows, annihilation that the Country wants, and not merely a splendid Victory of twenty-three to thirty-six,—honorable to the parties concerned, but absolutely useless in the extended scale to bring Buonaparte to his marrow-bones: numbers can only annihilate."

Written from HMS *Victory* to Sir George Rose, Nelson's friend and confidant of Prime Minister Pitt, October 1805

Nelson understood the impact of public opinion on politics. When he referred to the necessity of annihilating the French fleet, he showed his awareness of the importance of a major victory over the French fleet to public morale and the related public support for Pitt's government. Nelson's ability to achieve resounding victories at politically crucial times was one of the major factors in his phenomenal public popularity and the willingness of Whitehall and the Admiralty to overlook the troublesome aspects of his personal life.

"[N]o naval officer is able to form a reliable opinion
about the merits of a national army."
—C. S. Forester

6. Armies

❧

*"Armies go so slow, that Seamen think they never mean to get
forward; but I dare say they act on a surer principle, although
we seldom fail."*

Written from Bastia, Corsica, to Nelson's wife,
February 1794

By the time he was involved in the Corsican campaign, Nelson
had been commanding ships of the British navy for nearly fifteen
years. He had served in the Atlantic off the northeast coast of
America and in the West Indies, East Indies, Baltic, and Mediterranean. He had led the naval portion of the joint attack with the
British army on Fort San Juan in Nicaragua and had been
involved in the support of army operations in the Mediterranean.
Notwithstanding his extensive experience, Nelson suffered from
a parochial view of the navy's sister service. Ironically, Nelson's
subjectivity about armies was the companion to Napoleon's failure to understand the true capabilities and limits of his naval
forces.

Notwithstanding his patronizing attitude towards armies in general and the British army in particular, Nelson performed well as leader of the British naval support at Bastia. He maintained a blockade, provided shore bombardment, led commando-like raids, and established and led an artillery battery of naval guns that were moved ashore. He also vigorously urged a prompt attack on the town, a tactic that the British army resisted. The contrast between his own combat doctrine and that of the British army at Bastia reinforced Nelson's general antipathy towards armies.

∽

"Our battery will open in about two days. . . . I have little doubt of our success; and if we do, what a disgrace to the Fiorenzo wise-heads:—if we do not, it can only be owing to their neglect in not attacking the place with us."
Written from the British encampment near Bastia to his
uncle William Suckling, April 1794

A heavy bombardment of the town of Bastia, coupled with an amphibious landing to the town's north and the starvation of the defenders, precipitated its surrender. The bombardment was accomplished with naval guns that were established ashore, an impressive engineering feat, under Nelson's leadership. Nelson described the achievement as "a work of the greatest difficulty, and which never, in my opinion, would have been accomplished by any other than British seamen."

In August, a similar feat was accomplished during an attack on Calvi. During that bombardment and counter bombardment, Nelson was wounded by debris flung up by a French round shot that struck the breastworks protecting a British battery. The wound, which did not appear to be serious at the time, eventually cost Nelson the sight of his right eye. Suffering a different kind of pain, Nelson felt that his commander in chief,

Admiral Lord Hood, failed to give him full credit for his initiative and exceptional naval professionalism during the Corsica operations. It was one of many situations where Nelson felt he did not get appropriate credit for his combat accomplishments. It also was a situation marked by friction between the British navy and their British army counterparts, who were reluctant to mount the attack on Bastia before their reinforcements had arrived.

"The seamen are very healthy in comparison with the Army, who in a week will be half sick. I attribute our healthiness to our hard work, and quantity of wine allowed."

Written from the British encampment at Bastia to
Admiral Lord Hood, July 1794

Nelson's focus on the comparative health among Britain's army and navy forces at Calvi was a reflection of his proactive attitude toward maintaining the good health of his officers and men. He paid a great deal of attention to the health of the seamen in his commands, and his ships and squadrons were comparatively healthy in an era when sickness could—and often did—compromise the fighting effectiveness of a military unit.

"When Lord Hood quits this station, I should be truly sorry to remain; he is the greatest Sea-officer I ever knew; and what can be said against him, I cannot conceive, it must only be envy, and it is better to be envied than pitied. But this comes from the Army, who have also poisoned some few of our minds. The taking of Bastia, contrary to all Military judgment, is such an attack on them that it is never to be forgotten."

Written from HMS *Agamemnon* to his wife,
September 1794

With many combat victories, the aftermath is tainted by jealousies among the victorious principals; the Corsican campaign was one such. It also was unfortunate in that it solidified Nelson's negative opinions about the British army at a point shortly before he became a national hero.

∾

"I am not, Fanny, quite so well pleased as I expected with this Army, which is slow beyond all description; and I begin to think, that the Emperor is anxious to touch another four millions of English money."

Written from HMS *Agamemnon* in Vado Bay to his wife, September 1795

Nelson's low opinion of armies was not limited to the British army. In this letter he extends it to the Austrian army led by General de Vins, who lectured Nelson when he urged that the general consider an attack on St. Remo. The general observed "that in all enterprises it is necessary to calculate the advantages that would accrue, if entirely successful, or only partially so; and also the disadvantages that might arise, if it terminated unsuccessfully." One can only imagine Nelson's reaction to that bit of military thought.

In addition, De Vins also took the liberty of lecturing Nelson about the relative naval advantages of St. Remo and Vado, two of the ports along the Riviera that Nelson knew from extended experience. Nelson's comment about the Emperor's interest in English money relates to the substantial British subsidy that supported the Austrian's military efforts against France. Not surprisingly, in time de Vins was routed by the French army.

∾

"I beg you will endeavour to impress on those about the General, the necessity of punctuality in a joint operation, for its suc-

cess to be complete. . . . I do not mean this as any complaint, but to show the necessity of punctuality; for had the Austrians kept back, very few of the French could have escaped."
Written from HMS *Agamemnon* to Francis Drake,
British Envoy to Genoa, April 1796

The frustration that shows through in this letter has to do with the failure of the Austrian army, under General Beaulieu, to conform to the planned timing of an attack. The result was a missed opportunity for a British navy squadron to bombard the French troops as they withdrew along the Riviera coast. Nelson's admonition about timing shows that he understood how critical a factor it was in combined army-navy operations. On the other hand, the complaint also suggests that Nelson failed to understand an important similarity between land and sea warfare, namely that there was a high degree of unpredictability in combat in the field as well as in combat at sea.

"I am vain enough to think I could command on shore as well as some of the Generals I have heard of; but it is past. I shall always feel a glow of gratitude in reflecting on your kind and uniform opinion of my conduct."
Written from HMS *Agamemnon* in Genoa harbor to
John Trevor, British Minister at Turin, April 1796

Nelson was quick to point out that civilians and army officers did not understand the complexities of naval tactics and strategy. On the other hand, he did not hesitate to offer the opinion that he could do a better job than "some of the Generals." The second part of the statement is of particular interest, since Nelson had handled Trevor rather roughly in some of his correspondence with him.

～

"I suppose England will be the last to make peace; and whilst she trusts to her Wooden Walls, she will be more successful than any other Power. This has ever been proved, yet we continue blindly to be attached to an Army."

Written from HMS *Captain* to his brother, the
Reverend William Nelson, June 1796

Nelson had as firm a grip on broad national strategy as he did on naval combat tactics. His offhand comment to his brother would have been worthy of sea power philosopher-advocates to come, such as Britain's Julian Corbett and America's Alfred Thayer Mahan.

～

"The harmony and good understanding between the Army and Navy employed on this occasion, will I trust be a farther proof of what may be effected by the hearty co-operation of the two services."

Written from HMS *Captain* to Admiral Sir John Jervis,
July 1796

In 1796 things were not going well in the Mediterranean for the British. The French army of Italy had been turned over to Napoleon, who quickly gathered considerable military and political momentum among the monarchies in northern Italy, including the Grand Duchy of Tuscany. Against that background, the fortress town of Porto Ferrajo was perceived by the British as a potential jumping off point for a French effort to retake Corsica.

On 9 July of that year, Nelson wrote to his commander in chief, Admiral Sir John Jervis, from his anchorage off Porto Ferrajo. He reported receiving word the previous day from the British Viceroy of Corsica that a decision had been made to take possession of the town. On 10 July Nelson reported to Jervis that the joint army-navy mission of taking the town had been accomplished. The event, and Nelson's reaction to it, clearly suggests that his opinions, good or bad, about the British army, like many of his strong views, were based on results.

"Leghorn is, from all accounts last night, in such a state, that a respectable force landed, would, I have every reason to suppose, insure the immediate possession of the Town. . . . I well know the difficulty of getting a proper person to command this party. Firmness, and that the people of Leghorn should know the person commanding, will most assuredly have a great effect . . . we know the jealousy of the Army against the Navy."

Written from HMS *Captain* to Sir Gilbert Elliot,
British Viceroy of Corsica, August 1796

In this letter Nelson makes a blunt appeal for command of a joint operation. In addition to his reference to being known by the Leghornese, he cited the fact that he held a commission as colonel in the Royal Marines. Such cross-service commissions were largely honorary, with the additional benefit of enhancing the pay of the recipient. Nelson even went so far as to suggest the person who should be the senior officer under him in the operation. His proposal was complicated by the fact that his selection for second in command was not the senior army representative available.

From a subsequent letter to the viceroy, it appears that Nelson's self-nomination did not succeed.

"I have the honour to acquaint you that I arrived at Bastia on the 14th . . . the embarkation of provisions and stores commenced on the 15th, and was continued without intermission till the 19th at sunset. In that night every soldier and other person were

brought off with perfect good order. . . . The cordiality with which
the whole of this service was carried on between His Excellency
the Vice-Roy, Lieutenant-General de Burgh, and myself, I can-
not but think it right to inform you of."
> Written from HMS *Captain* to Admiral Sir John Jervis,
> October 1796

Although Nelson's inclination was towards the offense in military operations—and he had repeatedly evidenced negativism
towards the army—the evacuation of Bastia was a defensive,
combined operation that he executed superbly. In his official
dispatch, Jervis cited "the unwearied labour of Commodore Nelson." The operation, one of the last steps of the total British
naval withdrawal from the Mediterranean, had to be particularly onerous for Nelson. With a nice touch of historical drama,
it was Nelson who led the British navy back into the Mediterranean with a vengeance in 1798.

❧

"*[T]hey have not the same boldness in undertaking a political*
measure that we have; we look to the benefit of our Country,
and risk our own fame every day to serve her; a Soldier obeys
his orders, and no more."
> Written from HMS *Captain* to Admiral Lord St. Vincent,
> April 1797

This statement was part of a letter to Nelson's commander in
chief analyzing a plan for a possible amphibious assault against
Tenerife that had been advanced by the admiral. When the
army declined to provide troops for the attack, Nelson under-
took to make the assault with naval and ships' marine forces
alone. The result was a disaster.

❦

"You must think, of giving me 200 Marines in addition to what I can land; the whole business is arranged in my mind, and I can point out to you the absolute necessity. Captain Old-field is a very worthy man; and under General Troubridge ashore, and myself afloat, I am confident of success."

Written from HMS *Theseus* to Admiral Lord St. Vincent, June 1797

The flippant reference to Captain Troubridge as "General" was a clue to Nelson's dangerous underestimation of the enemy he was to meet at the Battle of Santa Cruz. The leader of the Spanish defense forces there, General Antonio Gutiérrez, was a highly professional army officer, and his skillful leadership during the battle was instrumental in inflicting a clear-cut defeat on Nelson and the British navy-marine force that attacked the city of Santa Cruz.[1] In addition to suffering the defeat in combat, Nelson lost his right arm when it was shattered above the elbow by enemy fire. The combination of the defeat and wound almost ended his career.

❦

"At 9 o'clock I was most agreeably surprised at the appearance of General Stuart, who has brought with him 1000 English Troops. This conduct of the General most assuredly demands the warmest gratitude from His Sicilian Majesty, and I have no doubt but he will experience it. This goodness of General Stuart reflects upon him the highest honour. He has probably, by his quick decision, not only saved this Kingdom, but may be the instrument of driving the French out of the Kingdom of Naples. It will be an electrical shock to the good and the bad."

Written from Palermo to Earl St. Vincent, March 1799

If Nelson often was critical of the British army's seeming inability to react quickly and decisively, he also was generous with his praise when a general made a quick decision that fit Nelson's aggressive combat approach.

"In January 1780, an Expedition being resolved on against St. Juan's, I was chosen to direct the Sea part of it. Major Polson, who commanded, will tell you of my exertions: how I quitted my Ship, carried troops in boats an hundred miles up a river, which none but Spaniards since the time of the buccaneers had ever ascended. It will then be told how I boarded, if I may be allowed the expression, an out-post of the Enemy . . . that I made batteries, and afterwards fought them, and was a principal cause of our success."

Written from HMS *Foudroyant,* at Port Mahon, Minorca,
to John M'Arthur, October 1799

These lines were part of a "Sketch of My Life" provided by Nelson at the request of John M'Arthur, who became a coauthor of one of the earliest serious Nelson biographies, *The Life of Admiral Lord Nelson,* published in 1809. Although the combined operation described by Nelson, which had taken place almost thirty years earlier, ultimately was not successful, it was an example of how energetically he could work with his British army compatriots when the personal chemistry was good.

In his official dispatch on the Fort San Juan operation, then–Major John Polson wrote of Nelson: "I want words to express the obligations I owe that gentleman. He was the first on every service whether by night or day."

❧

"I am sensible of General Palffy's flattering compliments, but as I cannot be a judge of the movements of an Army, so he cannot of that of a Fleet. He is either ignorant, or appears so, that the greatest Naval force of the Enemy is blocked up in Malta by our Ships."

Written from Palermo to William Wyndham,
British Minister at Florence, December 1799

Ever defensive about even implied criticism of himself or the British navy by an army officer, this rejoinder includes an additional element, his quickness to dismiss opinions by those who did not know a situation firsthand.

> "All people who have reached the point of
> becoming nations tend to despise foreigners."
> —George Orwell

7. Foreigners

~

"The Dons may make fine Ships,—they cannot, however, make men."

Written from HMS *Agamemnon* to his wife, June 1793

Two different points emerge from this comment, which was made after a visit to Cadiz and during a period of friendship between Britain and Spain. First, during Nelson's career, both the Spanish and the French apparently produced warships whose designs often were superior to those of the British. And in combat, it was the training and tactics of the British navy that consistently tipped the balance in their favor. The second point goes to the fact that Nelson apparently extended his belief in British fighting superiority to the Spanish army. At the Battle of Santa Cruz in 1797, that presumption cost him heavily. In that event, he was soundly beaten by the tough Castillian general, Antonio Gutiérrez. The Spaniard led the defense of Santa Cruz with high degrees of professionalism and determination. His preparation of his regular army and militia forces, and their deployment during the British attack, were as important as any other factor in Nelson's defeat.

∼

"The Allied Powers seem jealous of each other, and none but England is hearty in the cause."
Written from HMS *Agamemnon* in Genoa to his wife,
September 1794

When this letter was written, the French had taken possession of Vado Bay, an important base for Nelson's ships on the Riviera coast. With accuracy, Nelson believed that the enthusiasm among the small kingdoms of the region for standing up to the French was considerably less than his own. The strategic importance of Britain's allies—or at the very least its nominal friends—in the Mediterranean was something that he clearly understood. And with that understanding came a chronic frustration with their reluctance to resist the French political and military incursions in the area.

∼

"Our Allies are our burden. Had we left the Continent to themselves, we should have done well, and half the expense."
Written from HMS *Agamemnon* in Leghorn to his uncle
William Suckling, October 1794

Nelson was well aware of the reality that Britain subsidized many of her foreign allies, a practice not unknown to the major world powers of today. His straightforward opinion of this eighteenth-century version of foreign military aid is the view of a naval officer who had to judge his allies on the basis of their willingness to fight and their effectiveness in combat.

"The rascality of Neutral Powers we all know."
Written from HMS *Agamemnon* in Leghorn to his uncle
William Suckling, November 1794

In 1794 the military tide was beginning to run against the British
in the Mediterranean. In December 1793 the French republicans
had retaken Toulon from the French monarchists who briefly
had held the city with British support, and Spain was edging
closer to an alliance with France. The small nations of northern Italy were looking with greater concern in the direction of
France. In this letter, Nelson's anger was focused on Denmark
and Sweden for shipping timber to Toulon, or to Genoa and to
Leghorn, where it was transshipped to France.

*"I know of no Country so pleasant to serve in as this, or where
my health is so good."*
Written from HMS *Agamemnon* at Leghorn to his father,
September 1795

In later years, Nelson's comments about the region of northern
Italy were less complimentary, particularly after his victory at the
Battle of the Nile.

*"In the opinion of the Genoese, my Squadron is constantly
offending; so that it almost appears a trial between us, who
shall first be tired, they of complaining, or me of answering
them. However, my mind is fixed; and nothing they can say
will make me alter my conduct towards them."*
Written from HMS *Agamemnon* in Vado Bay to his wife,
October 1795

Nelson's sense of duty, stubbornness, and predilection for action created difficulties for him in his relations with the small states of northern Italy. The weak governments there were attempting to tread a narrow line between the French and the British, and did not appreciate his unequivocal opposition to any and all French military or political moves.

"My situation with this Army has convinced me, by ocular demonstration, of the futility of Continental Alliances. The conduct of the Court of Vienna, whatever may be said by the House of Commons to the contrary, is nothing but deception."
Written from HMS *Agamemnon* off Marseilles to his uncle
William Suckling, October 1795

Although Nelson was capable of grasping grand strategy, he also was capable of forming narrowly focused, negative opinions on the basis of his own first-hand observations of how Britain's allies—or potential allies—performed when threatened by French armies. Establishing and maintaining alliances was an important element of Britain's basic strategy during Nelson's career. However, Nelson saw firsthand how, in this instance, the Austrian military commanders and their army in northern Italy performed in the field. He was not impressed, and it strongly colored his opinion of Britain's alliance with Austria. The situation was a classic example of the disconnect that often exists between a nation's military commanders in a combat theater and their distant political leadership.

"[A]ll Frenchmen are alike; I despise them all. They are (even those who are fed by us) false and treacherous: even Louis XVIII

receives our money, and will not follow our advice, and keep
up the dignity of the King of France at Verona."
Written from HMS *Agamemnon* off Marseilles to his uncle
William Suckling, October 1795

In the same letter in which he complained about Continental
alliances, Nelson had some harsh words for Britain's French
antagonists. It was a theme he repeated often in his correspondence. Later, his dislike and distrust of the French were to be
sharply focused on Napoleon and French republicanism.

Louis XVIII, who briefly took the throne of France when
Napoleon abdicated in 1814 and again when Napoleon was
defeated at Waterloo in 1815, was supported by British subsidies.
At this point in time, Nelson still held out hope that the monarchy could be restored in France.

"We have established the French Republic, which, but for us, I
verily believe would never have been settled by such a volatile,
changeable people. I hate a Frenchman. They are equally objects
of my detestation, whether Royalists or Republicans—in some
points, I believe the latter are the best."
Written from HMS *Agamemnon* at Leghorn to his friend, the
Reverend Dixon Hoste, December 1795

In this letter, Nelson did not elaborate on what points the French
republicans were better than their royalist counterparts. But over
time, his letters and dispatches reveal that his antipathy toward
republicanism grew to match his general dislike for the French.

"I very much believe that England, who commenced the war
with all Europe for her Allies, will finish it by having nearly
all Europe for her Enemies."
Written from HMS *Agamemnon* to Sir Gilbert Elliot,
British Viceroy of Corsica, May 1796

This reflection of a broad cynicism about Britain's foreign allies was part of Nelson's diplomatic and military analysis of the situations in Sardinia, Corsica, and the Kingdom of Tuscany. The letter, which includes comments on the larger strategic issues involved in that theater of operations, demonstrates how important the British navy and officers like Nelson were as intelligence-gathering sources for Britain's political leaders. The letter also is one of the best examples of Nelson's willingness to push his opinions about foreign affairs that related to naval situations with which he was involved. As it turned out, events in Europe after Nelson's death bore out his sweeping prediction.

"In short, Italy has been lost by the fears of its Princes; had they expended half the money to preserve their Territories, which they have paid the French for entering them, their Countries would have been happy, instead of being filled with present misery and diabolical notions of Government."
Written from HMS *Captain* to his friend, Captain William Locker, Lieutenant Governor of Greenwich Naval Hospital, November 1796

This letter reflects Nelson's contempt for the rulers of Corsica and the small kingdoms of northern Italy. In July 1796, Napoleon had taken over the French army of Italy, and by October the British had been forced to withdraw from Corsica. In addition, other ports in northern Italy, such as Leghorn, were denied to the British navy. In a futile attempt to protect Corsica, a squadron led by Nelson had occupied Elba in July. However, in December, the British withdrew from there as well, eliminating their naval presence in the Mediterranean altogether.

⤳

*"I cannot allow Don Jacobo to return to you without express-
ing my admiration of his gallant conduct."*
Written from HMS *La Minerve* to Admiral Don Juan Marino,
December 1796

Don Jacobo Stuart was the captain of the Spanish ship *Santa
Sabina,* which Nelson had captured in a single-ship action. However, the *Santa Sabina,* with the British prize crew aboard, was
quickly recaptured by the Spanish. Stuart had fought his ship
bravely, and Nelson demonstrated the respect he had for a for-
eigner who also was a valiant opponent in combat. His letter offered Stuart in a prisoner exchange for two British navy lieutenants
who had been taken during the recapture of the *Santa Sabina.* In
his letter, Nelson articulated an important part of his warrior's
code—generous conduct towards a defeated enemy who fought
bravely—which he followed in victory and benefited from in defeat.

⤳

*"I do not build much on the acts of the Portuguese Squadron,
even if they go off Spartel."*
Written from HMS *Theseus* to Admiral Earl St. Vincent,
his commander in chief, June 1797

The reference to the Portuguese Squadron came at the very end of
a dispatch to St. Vincent, and it reflected a general opinion by Nelson that the ships and squadrons of Britain's foreign allies were,
generally, of little help. The Portuguese admiral, the Marquis De
Niza, commanded the squadron in question, and subsequent correspondence indicates that Nelson had a low opinion not only of
the Portuguese squadron, but of its commander as well. However,
based on later events, those opinions, particularly that about De
Niza, improved considerably. Making premature negative judgments about people was one of Nelson's characteristics. His ability to publicly modify those judgments in the light of events was
one of his strengths.

~

"I cannot take my departure from this Island, without returning your Excellency my sincerest thanks for your attention towards me, by your humanity in favor of our wounded men in your power, or under your care, and for your generosity towards all our people who were disembarked, which I shall not fail to represent to my Sovereign. . . . I trust your Excellency will do me the honour to accept of a Cask of English beer and a cheese."
Written from HMS *Theseus* in Santa Cruz harbor to General Antonio Gutiérrez, commander of the Spanish defenses of Tenerife, July 1797

This gallant statement to his victorious adversary followed the crushing repulse of Nelson's amphibious assault on Santa Cruz between 22–24 July 1797. During the landing on Santa Cruz's mole, Nelson's right arm was shattered in a hail of Spanish fire, and he was immediately returned to *Theseus* where his arm was amputated. The message to the victorious Gutiérrez was among the first documents signed by Nelson with his left hand. General Gutiérrez's response to Nelson was equally gallant.

Nelson's message sharply illuminated one of his most noteworthy personal qualities. Despite his tendency to look disapprovingly on many foreigners, he did not extend his dislike to those military opponents whom he considered courageous and honorable. This humane quality stood in bold relief against his ferocity in combat, creating one of the more striking contrasts in his personality.

~

"We have saved Sicily in spite of Neapolitan councils. That Marquis de Gallo is a wretch who minds nothing but fine clothes, his snuff-box, and ring; this is the best I can say of him."
Written from HMS *Vanguard* off Rhodes to Lord Minto, former Viceroy of Corsica, August 1798

One of Nelson's biographers described De Gallo, Secretary of State for the Kingdom of the Two Sicilies, as "shifty, effeminate and anti-British." Given Nelson's personality, and his opinion of foreign court politicians in general, one can understand his contempt for such a person.

~

"I have heard nothing of the Portuguese. I do not find any person here very anxious for their return to Naples. . . . [T]he whole of my conduct and that of the Portuguese, is considered as the difference between impudence and modesty."

Written from HMS *Vanguard* in Naples harbor to
Admiral Earl St. Vincent, September 1798

In an informationally rich report to his commander in chief, Nelson touches on one of the basic issues for naval forces: how they are perceived by the officials and populace in their foreign host ports. Nelson's use of the word "modesty" in connection with his conduct has to create smiles. However, it does clearly indicate that he understood that there was a direct correlation between his official behavior in Naples and the relationship between Britain and the Kingdom of the Two Sicilies.

~

"I trust, my Lord, in a week we shall be at sea. I am very unwell, and the miserable conduct of this Court is not likely to cool my irritable temper. It is a country of fiddlers and poets, whores and scoundrels."

Written from Naples to Admiral Earl St. Vincent,
September 1798

This three-sentence message to Nelson's commander in chief speaks volumes. When Nelson returned to Naples after his strategically critical victory over the French battle fleet at the

Battle of the Nile in August of 1798, he was celebrated as the savior, not only of the Kingdom of the Two Sicilies, but of all Europe. The celebrations of his victory, and the personal praise that was heaped upon him personally, were exorbitant. It also was a time when he was just beginning to recover from a head wound that showed all the symptoms of a dangerously serious concussion. Further compounding the circumstances, it is almost certain that it was during this time that his romantic relationship with Lady Hamilton began.

It is not difficult to imagine how Nelson saw his return to the routine of an underway British warship and the requirements of his naval profession as relief from the emotional turbulence and social excesses in the Court at Naples. His friend and brother officer, Thomas Troubridge, had an even stronger reaction to the Naples scene when he wrote, "God send I may never see this degenerate place again."

❦

"The Marquis deserves credit for his perseverance, but his Ships cannot do what ours can."
Written from HMS *Vanguard* in Naples to Admiral Earl St. Vincent, December 1798

Nelson's attitude toward the Marquis De Niza had moderated at this point. But his recognition that the operational performance of the Portuguese squadron De Niza commanded was not on a par with the British navy was still clearly apparent.

❦

"[T]he Russians seem to me to be more intent on taking Ports in the Mediterranean than destroying Buonaparte in Egypt."
Written from HMS *Vanguard* to Admiral Earl St. Vincent, December 1798

The securing of Mediterranean ports had been a goal of Russian leaders for centuries, and Nelson recognized that ongoing reality in his theater of operations. His brief observation in his report to St. Vincent was another piece of evidence proving that his grasp of strategic issues went beyond his immediate duties.

❧

"I am here solus, for I reckon the Portuguese as nothing. They are all Flag-Officers and cannot serve under my brave friends!"
Written from Naples to Commodore Sir John Duckworth,
December 1798

Nelson's complaint reflects a special problem of combined operations. On the one hand, he commanded a group of British captains who were both courageous and skilled. He had the utmost confidence in this Band of Brothers that was battle tested. On the other hand, he was working with a Portuguese squadron whose commanders, despite technically being senior in rank to Nelson's captains, from his perspective did not have the capabilities of those men.

❧

"The situation of this Country is very critical—nearly all in it are traitors or cowards."
Written from Naples to Captain Alexander Ball—
December 1798

This letter was written at a testing time for Nelson. He had sent Ball to blockade the French forces that had taken Malta as Napoleon was on his way to Egypt. He himself remained in Naples to assure the protection of Britain's ally, the Kingdom of the Two Sicilies. Increasingly, many, including both friends and supporters, believed that he was drawn to Naples because of his romantic attachment to Lady Hamilton and her strong influence on him.

At the time this letter was written, Napoleon's army of Italy, and the very real possibility of an insurrection, threatened the Kingdom of the Two Sicilies. Understandably, that combination of circumstances brought his basic distrust of most foreigners to the fore. Within weeks, Nelson was forced to carry out the evacuation of the Neapolitan court from Naples to Palermo.

～

"[W]e must never suffer an insult to pass unpunished."
Written from HMS *Foudroyant* to Perkin Magra,
British Consul at Tunis, June 1799

Just as he developed a simple combat doctrine for his battles, Nelson had the equivalent for diplomatic matters.

～

"There is no way of dealing with a Frenchman but to knock him down. To be civil to them is only to be laughed at, when they are enemies."
Written from HMS *Foudroyant* in Naples Bay to
Captain Thomas Louis, HMS *Minotaur,* August 1799

When the pro-French Neapolitans and the French occupiers of Naples were defeated, Nelson summarily annulled a truce that had been signed with one group and angrily demanded that Captain Louis, and others involved, accept nothing but complete capitulation. Once the capitulation had been secured to his satisfaction, Nelson added this admonition to his captain about how to deal with a Frenchman. It was another of the many expressions of his particular hatred for the French.

～

"I am obliged to send Niza to co-operate with you in the reduction of Malta. He is a good young man, and will afford you every assistance."
Written from Palermo to Captain Alexander Ball,
August 1799

The blockade of Malta had an extremely high priority for Nelson and sending De Niza to assist Ball was evidence of rising confidence in the young Portuguese admiral, notwithstanding Nelson's concerns about having a technically senior foreign admiral operating under the de facto leadership of one of his Band of Brothers. To the credit of Ball and De Niza, they appear to have worked things out.

"The Russian Admiral has a polished outside, but the bear is close to the skin. He is jealous of our influence, and thinks whatever is proposed, that we are at the bottom. The Turk, who is by no means a fool—on the contrary, has more natural sense than the other—is our brother; and I am sure there is not a thing that we could desire him to do that he would not instantly comply with. I make use of the word 'we,' as both Sir William and Lady Hamilton have more merit in gaining the affection and implicit confidence of Cadir Bey and his Officers, than I have."

Written from Palermo to Earl Spencer, First Lord of the Admiralty, September 1799

This psycho-political analysis reflects Nelson's deep involvement at the time with the royal court of the Kingdom of the Two Sicilies, where he was ensconced. He seems to be more involved in the political aspects of the naval struggle against Napoleon than with the military issues. It is as if he was, for a time, caught up in the kind of court maneuverings he so detested. It was a radical change, albeit brief, in his warrior's style.

"Your Excellency's conduct as an Officer and a man, in every situation, has been most grateful to my feelings; but your con-

duct since you have been off Malta, will stamp your character as a Sea-officer, second to none in Europe. If it is of any value, you have my warmest gratitude for your support of me on every occasion."

Written from Palermo to the Marquis De Niza,
November 1799

Nelson's relationship with the Portuguese admiral had shifted 180 degrees. The Marquis had carried out Nelson's orders in a professional manner, and had even defied his government's orders to return to Lisbon to stay on blockade duty at Malta. The latter was the kind of political courage that had to endear him to Nelson. Today, Lisbon's Museu de Marinha proudly displays memorabilia from De Niza's service with Nelson in the Mediterranean, along with portraits of the two men.

"All the folks are thieves, and think us fair game."

Written from HMS *St. George* in Revel Bay to
Admiral Earl St. Vincent, May 1801

Revel, now known as Tallinn, is located on the coast of the Gulf of Finland in Estonia. At the time, it was part of Russia. Nelson was there, following his victory at the Battle of Copenhagen, as the commander in chief of Britain's Baltic fleet. His comment about the character of the "folks" came as an afterthought in the message to St. Vincent, who had become the First Lord of the Admiralty. Complaints about the treatment of a naval force during a port visit are a constant that stretches over time and nationalities. Even today, naval ships and their sailors are a welcome source of income in the foreign ports they visit, but the hospitality of the hosts is often colored by a "let the buyer beware" attitude.

"Forgive me; but my mother hated the French."
Written from HMS *Victory* to Hugh Elliot,
British Ambassador at Naples, October 1803

In an instance where Nelson's last lines of a letter were particularly revealing, he identifies the roots of his antipathy towards the French.

"[T]he great attention and ready release which our prisoners have met with from the Spanish Government, deserve on our part a liberal return."
Written from HMS *Victory* to William Marsden,
First Secretary to the Admiralty, March 1805

During this time, Nelson was involved in an exchange of French and Spanish prisoners held at Malta for British prisoners held in Cadiz. In this particular instance, his previous experiences with the humane actions of the Spanish towards prisoners of war were reinforced, and his warrior's code was still intact as his career neared its climax at Cape Trafalgar.

> "He who commands the sea has command
> of everything."
> —Themistocles

8. Sea Power

~

*"This traffic . . . brings to the King of Spain a considerable rev-
enue; it will increase the Ship-building of America, and raise
the numbers of her Sea-men, while, on the contrary, it will
decrease the British Shipping and Seamen in these Islands."*
Written from HMS *Boreas* at English Harbor, Antigua, to
Philip Stephens, Secretary to the Admiralty, August 1786

This comment was part of a long report to the Admiralty on
how American ships were becoming, through subterfuge,
"Spanish" ships while in the West Indies. In this way they were
sidestepping Britain's Navigation Acts, which among other
things, were designed to prevent the newly independent America from direct trading in the British West Indies. The essence
of the report was that Nelson was going to do everything in his
power to hinder the trade, despite the fact that British merchants and officials in the area were more interested in their
profits than in the laws.

Nelson's rather stiff-necked attitude was more than a desire to force adherence to a law for its own sake. Despite his youth (he had not yet reached thirty years of age), Nelson clearly understood the complex interrelationships between different facets of sea power and was acting on that basis. He understood that sea power was more than warships and naval battles, and he pursued his duty, even at the risk of his career, in the context of Britain's broad maritime interests.

"The loss to the French has been great indeed: all the Ships built at Toulon have their sides, beams, decks, and straight timbers from this Island. The pine of this Island is of the finest texture I ever saw; and the tar, pitch, and hemp, although I believe the former not equal to Norway, yet were very much used in the yard at Toulon."

> Written from HMS *Agamemnon* at St. Fiorenzo, Corsica, to his uncle William Suckling, February 1795

Naval stores were extremely critical strategic materials during Britain's wars against Napoleon. In addition to Corsica's potential role as a geographically important naval base, Nelson recognized the double strategic benefit of denying the naval stores of the island to the French and securing them for Britain's Mediterranean operations.

"The Enemy have a great many small Privateers at sea, and many of our Merchant-ships are taken."

> Written from HMS *Agamemnon* at Leghorn to his uncle William Suckling, May 1795

During Nelson's career, British sea trade was vulnerable to privateers, notwithstanding her generally effective naval forces.

Convoys mitigated the problem, but never totally eliminated this threat to the commercial life blood of the empire. Privateering, as a form of naval warfare, was considered unworthy by many, including Nelson. He once described British privateers as "a disgrace to our Country." However, he understood the threat of privateers to Britain's trade and financial viability, two essential elements of her national strength.

"We are sorry to hear such very bad accounts from the coast of Brittany, but somehow on shore we have never been successful for a continuance (of) this war."

Written from HMS *Agamemnon* at Vado Bay between Nice and Genoa to J. Harriman, Clerk to the British Consul at Leghorn, August 1795

This reference to a failed British expedition at Quiberon focuses on a basic fact of the struggle between Britain and France at the end of the eighteenth century: sea power was Britain's principal military instrument of foreign policy.

"What would then have been said when the French had been riding triumphant on the seas, as I fear they are on the land? I will tell you:—'England was bound to keep a Fleet equal to cope with the Enemy in the Mediterranean; the Admiral, to take a few prizes, has lost his Fleet'. . . . Our Fleet, thank God, is perfect, and if the enemy will give us an opportunity, the ancient glory of the British navy will be kept up. I need not enlarge on this subject. You will, at proper times and places, make a proper use of it."

Written from HMS *Agamemnon* in the Gulf of Genoa to John Trevor, British Minister at Turin, April 1796

This minilecture to a British diplomat was additional evidence of Nelson's sensitivity to criticism of the British navy, and more importantly, showed his grasp of the broad implications of sea power. It was in response to apparent criticism of the British navy's actions in not attacking a convoy.

Earlier in this letter, Nelson alluded to the criticism harshly, "Nothing but their ignorance of Sea affairs can palliate, but by no means excuse them, giving their opinion on a professional subject of which they must be totally ignorant." In a transparent effort to add the authority of his commander in chief to his own remarks, Nelson added, "close to the Victory," at the opening of the letter. While it is easy to assume that the tone of the letter was not appreciated by the minister, the validity of Nelson's comments would have been difficult to contest.

"You may rest assured I shall afford every protection in my power to preserve the property of the English Merchants, and others, our allies; and act in other matters to the best of my judgment, and as circumstances may point out to me to be proper."

Written from HMS *Captain* at Genoa Mole to
Admiral Sir John Jervis, June 1796

This comment was one of many that demonstrated Nelson's understanding that the effective use of sea power involves a lot more than winning sea battles. In this case, he focused on the importance of Britain's merchant class. During the previous 200 years the rising merchant classes of Holland and Britain were engines for the development of a new political and intellectual environment.

It also is interesting that he chose to once again express his determination, this time to his commander in chief, to act on the basis of his own judgment and local circumstances in carrying out his duty.

"[T]he more I can anchor in sight of the place, the more effect it will have."
> Written from HMS *Captain* to Admiral Sir John Jervis,
> July 1796

At times, "showing the flag" is a cost-effective use of sea power. In this instance, Nelson hoped that the visible presence of his ships would contribute towards an insurrection of the local populace against the French occupiers of the area. It is another example of his grasp of, and ability to employ, the unique repertoire of sea power.

≈

"The French having possessed themselves of Malta . . . I think their object is, to possess themselves of some Port in Egypt, and to fix themselves at the head of the Red Sea, in order to get a formidable Army into India; and, in concert with Tippoo Saib, to drive us, if possible, from India."
> Written from HMS *Vanguard* to George Baldwin,
> British consul at Alexandria, June 1798

When this assessment was written, it was a difficult time for Nelson. He had unsuccessfully been searching the Mediterranean for Napoleon's invasion fleet. His luck had been embarrassingly bad, and he had just missed intercepting Napoleon at sea. However, once he learned that Napoleon had taken Malta, his assessment, built on a full understanding of sea power, was amazingly accurate. The port in Egypt that was Napoleon's object was Alexandria, and his long-range goal indeed was to threaten the British in India.

Fortunately for Britain, the French battle fleet was located and destroyed by Nelson at Aboukir Bay on 1 August 1798, and Napoleon's plan to get at British power through India was thwarted.

Nelson's application of sea power to isolate the French army in Egypt check-mated Napoleon's plans to threaten Britain economic resources in the Far East. *The Battle of the Nile, August 21, 1798;* engraving by J. Fittler from a painting by Nicholas Pocock.

"Was I to die this moment, 'Want of Frigates' would be found stamped on my heart."
> Written from HMS *Vanguard* at the mouth of the Nile to Earl Spencer, First Lord of the Admiralty, August 1798

Frigates were the work horses and "the eyes of the fleet" in Nelson's time, and his nerve-racking hunt for Napoleon leading up the Battle of the Nile was seriously hindered by the fact that he had lost touch with the four British frigates in the Mediterranean. It was a classic example of how the lack of adequate numbers of ships to carry out a naval force's mission can be expensive to a nation in the long run.

∾

"The French Army is in a scrape. They are up the Nile without supplies."
Written from HMS Vanguard to Alexander Davison,
his friend, August 1798

Although Nelson would dearly have loved to catch Napoleon and his fleet at sea, he knew that the destruction of the French battle fleet at Aboukir Bay, although less dramatic, also meant the eventual failure of Napoleon's master plan of attacking Britain through her East Indies possessions. From a strategic perspective, Nelson had administered a heavy blow to Napoleon and France at the Battle of the Nile, and he knew it. His two-sentence summation of the strategic situation to his friend, written only ten days after the Battle of the Nile, was one of many colorful examples of Nelson's ability with the written word.

∾

"[I]t is my duty, and it is my inclination to do everything for the protection of our commerce, consistent with the other important duties required of me."
Written from Palermo to William Wyndham,
British Minister at Florence, March 1799

The huge spectrum of potential actions encompassed by the various elements of sea power is, at times, one of the problems inherent in the use of this instrument of national power. On the same day that Nelson wrote to Wyndham, he reported to his commander in chief how the twenty-four ships of his squadron were deployed. Their disposition included the blockade of Alexandria, the blockade of Malta, convoy duty, refitting, and transit to and from various assignments—a testing operating tempo for only two dozen ships in a theater.

The ships and crews of Nelson's Mediterranean squadron were stretched to the limit. Both men and ships were severely stressed, but the special dedication and professionalism of the former maintained a finely honed force that effectively carried out a wide variety of missions on behalf of Britain's political leadership.

"It is our duty to take care of the Smyrna trade, as well all other, and it never has yet been neglected; but Great Britain, extensive as her Navy is, cannot afford to have one Ship lay idle."
Written from Palermo to Captain Sir Sidney Smith,
HMS *Tigre,* August 1799

Although Smyrna, now called Izmir, was an important port in Mediterranean trade, Nelson rightly pointed out that the British navy had too many demands on it to respond to a local request, apparently made through Smith, that a ship be allocated for the protection of that port. Smith had the unusual distinction of status as a British navy captain with official diplomatic standing. And Nelson resented the fact that a junior captain in his theater had an official political standing that, in some ways, placed him outside his authority. However, in this letter, he wrote in polite, if restrained, terms. To others, he complained in stronger terms about Smith's unusual status.

"I want Peace, which is only to be had through, I trust, our still invincible Navy."
Written from HMS *St. George* at Portsmouth to Admiral Earl
St. Vincent, First Lord of the Admiralty, March 1801

As he wrote to St. Vincent, Nelson was preparing to embark on a classic application of sea power. As second in command of a fleet being deployed to the Baltic to bring military pressure to bear on Denmark, he would exercise a dramatic combination of naval power and personal diplomacy. As a result of his combat leadership and blunt negotiating, Nelson precipitated the collapse of the League of Armed Neutrality, an alliance of Baltic nations that threatened both Britain's commercial trade and preeminence at sea.[1]

"I hope, we shall be able as usual to get so close to our Enemies that our shot cannot miss their object, and that we shall again give our Northern Enemies that hail-storm of bullets . . . which gives our dear Country the Dominion of the Seas. We have it, and all the Devils in hell cannot take it from us, if our Wooden walls have fair play."

Written from HMS *St. George* at Yarmouth to his friend, Captain Sir Edward Berry, March 1801

In this quick note to his friend, Edward Berry, Nelson illuminates the lethal end of the sea power instrument. The British navy's battle tactics of the time, applied repeatedly by Nelson with brilliant success, included getting near enough to the enemy for a close-in, smashing battle. The rapid fire of the British ships in those close quarters generally carried the day.

The reference to the British navy as Britain's wooden walls dates back at least to Thomas Coventry who, in 1635, addressed the House of Commons: "The dominion of the sea . . . is the best security of the land. The wooden walls are the best walls of this kingdom."

"[I]t is, therefore, necessary that all good men should come forward on this momentous occasion to oppose the Enemy, and, more particularly, the Sea-Fencibles, who have voluntarily enrolled themselves to defend their Country afloat, which is the

*true place where Britain ought to be defended. . . . Our Coun-
try looks to its Sea defence, and let it not be disappointed."*
  Written from HMS *Medusa* off Calais to Captains Shield,
          Hamilton, Schomberg, and Edge, August 1801

This ringing exhortation, delivered when Nelson was in command of the British anti-invasion force in the Channel, sounds
eerily like something from Britain's early World War II years. It
shows that there are timeless verities involved in the applications
of sea power in national conflicts.

*"I now declare, that I consider Malta as a most important out-
work to India, that it will ever give us great influence in the
Levant, and indeed all the Southern parts of Italy."*
        Written from HMS *Amphion* to Henry Addington,
                     Prime Minister, June 1803

Nelson's reference to Malta is part of a long situation analysis
that also included detailed comments on Gibraltar, Algiers,
Sicily, Sardinia, Rome, Tuscany, Genoa, and the Morea (southern peninsula of the Greek mainland). It is one of the best
examples of how Nelson saw beyond tactics and battles to the
broad strategic implications of sea power. Malta, for example,
was not simply seen as a matter of territorial acquisition for
Britain and denial for France. It was properly perceived as being
related to southern Italy, the eastern Mediterranean area that
today includes Syria and Lebanon, and even India. To a significant degree, Nelson's understanding of sea power was a precursor to the later sea power–philosophers to come, like America's Alfred Thayer Mahan and Britain's Julian Corbett.

～

"I would earnestly recommend that Genoa should be declared a Blockaded Port, and thus cut off all supplies for the Southern parts of France and the Northern parts of Italy."
Written from HMS *Amphion* to Sir Evan Nepean,
Secretary to the Admiralty, July 1803

Blockade is one of the less dramatic means of applying sea power, and it was frequently used with good effect by the British navy of Nelson's time. Blockade was hard, grinding duty that wore down both ships and crews, but it clearly was a serious military and economic hindrance to France at the time. During the latter eighteenth and early nineteenth centuries, a blockade was frequently applied by Britain but almost never by France, a demonstration of the differences between the two nations, both in terms of naval operational capability and a strategic understanding of sea power.

～

"Prevention is better than cure."
Written from HMS *Victory* off Toulon to Henry Addington,
Prime Minister, August 1803

In five words, one of history's most celebrated combat leaders summed up an important underlying argument for sea power: it can prevent war.

～

"I must not, in our present state, quarrel with the North Westers—with crazy masts and no Port or spars near us."
Written from HMS *Victory* off Toulon to Sir Alexander Ball,
Governor of Malta, September 1803

Naval bases and naval stores were both critical to Britain's application of sea power in the Mediterranean, and at times Nelson was seriously short of both. He refers to that reality in his letter to Ball, one of his Band of Brothers, by pointing out how he had to avoid the frequent storms from the northwest. It was a very practical factor that hindered his operational capabilities.

⤳

"God knows, if we could possess one Island, Sardinia, we should want neither Malta, nor any other."
                              Written from HMS *Victory* off Toulon to Lord Hobart,
                                              Secretary of War, December 1803

Strategically located naval bases are an essential element of sea power, and for Nelson, that was an ongoing problem in the Mediterranean. As French military control in the theater flowed and ebbed, his problem was exacerbated or mitigated. In this letter to a key Whitehall official, Nelson pointed out that Sardinia possessed "Harbours fit for Arsenals . . . within twenty-four hour's sail of Toulon." The latter point was an important practical factor that related to Nelson's ability to maintain an all-weather, all-seasons blockade of that strategically crucial port.

⤳

"I consider the protection of our Trade the most essential service that can be performed."
                      Written from HMS *Victory* to Captain Benjamin Hallowell,
                                                          HMS *Argo*, March 1804

The mercantilist policies of the British government of Nelson's time required not only very active foreign trade, but a favorable balance of that trade whereby Britain exported more than it imported. Thus, both the quantity and the quality of foreign trade were issues of great national importance. Correctly, Nelson saw that trade was both an element of sea power and the foundation of Britain's economic and military strength.

"I was in a thousand fears for Jamaica, for that is a blow which Buonaparte would be happy to give us. I flew to the West Indies without any orders, but I think the Ministry cannot be displeased."
Written from HMS *Victory* to Simon Taylor,
his friend in the West Indies, June 1805

After months of hunting a French fleet led by Admiral Villeneuve in the Mediterranean, Nelson learned that the fleet had headed for the West Indies. Although his theater of command responsibility was the Mediterranean, Nelson realized that if Villeneuve were free to attack Jamaica and other British West Indian colonies, it would be a serious economic blow to Britain. In order to checkmate this use of the flexibility of sea power by the French, he decided to pursue Villeneuve and prevent his mounting any serious attacks against the British in the West Indies. It was a decision that grew from Nelson's proactive nature and appreciation for the global reach of sea power. This also was an example of a strategic aggressiveness that matched Nelson's aggressive combat doctrine and tactics.

"I have had much communication with His Majesty's Ministers upon the subject of preventing Sardinia from falling into the hands of the French, which will be a severe blow upon us, for in that case, if the Enemy's Fleet get into Toulon, all the British Force in the Mediterranean must be occupied in turning them out of it, that our Fleet might have a place to resort to in order to watch Toulon, but I much fear that at this moment it may be lost."
Written from HMS *Victory* to Sir Alexander John Ball,
Governor of Malta, October 1805

When this letter was written, the Battle of Trafalgar—and a radical, permanent change in the strategic positions of France and Britain in the Mediterranean—was only weeks away. Nelson had thoroughly briefed his captains on his combat doctrine for the forthcoming battle with the combined French-Spanish fleet. However, despite the imminence of battle, he was still mindful of the importance of strategically located naval bases and how timing played importantly in bringing sea power to bear.

"I verily believe the Country will soon be put to some expense for my account, either a Monument, or a new Pension and Honours; for I have not the very smallest doubt but that a very few days, almost hours, will put us in Battle. . . . [A]nd I want for the sake of our Country that it should be done so effectually as to have nothing to wish for."

Written from HMS *Victory* near Cape Trafalgar to
Sir George Rose, friend and Vice President of the
British Board of Trade, October 1805

One of the most important changes in sea power during Nelson's time was the way naval battles were perceived. Previously, battles rarely involved the total defeat of the loser. Towards the end of the eighteenth century that changed, and Nelson was arguably the primary instrument of that change. At the Battle of the Nile both his combat doctrine and tactics were shaped to wipe out the opponent, and the French fleet was very decisively defeated. At Trafalgar, the approach, and result, were similar.

This change in how naval battles were perceived was shared by both Nelson and Britain's political leaders at Whitehall, a noteworthy example of agreement between the two. In the same letter, Nelson summed up the political situation before the Battle of Trafalgar, "[I]t is, as Mr. Pitt knows, annihilation that the

Country wants, and not merely a splendid Victory of twenty-three to thirty-six,—honourable to the parties concerned, but absolutely useless in the extended scale to bring Buonaparte to his marrow-bones: numbers only can annihilate."

Nelson and his prime minister both knew that the old style "moral victory" would not do in the context of Britain's use of sea power as its primary weapon of war against Napoleon. Only a crushing victory would do, and that is what Nelson purchased with his life.

"Let gentle blood show generous might. . . ."
—Sir Walter Scott

9. A Good Heart

~

"To be the messenger of bad news is my misfortune, but still it is a tribute that friends owe each other. I have lost my friend, and you an affectionate brother. . . . If the tribute of tears are valuable, my friend had them."
Written from HMS *Boreas* at Nevis to then–Captain
Cuthbert Collingwood, May 1787

A trendy and cynical characterization of the warrior's profession is that it is a job requiring one to "kill people and break things." Undeniably, Nelson was exceptionally good at those tasks. Yet, he consistently showed genuine sensitivity towards others. This letter to his brother officer is an example of that characteristic. He and Cuthbert Collingwood were friends from their time as junior officers, and when Collingwood's brother, Wilfred, commander of HMS *Rattler,* died, Nelson had the difficult duty of informing his friend of his brother's death.

This eloquent letter was much more than an official notification. It revealed Nelson's genuine grief and the respect that he had for Wilfred Collingwood. It was typical of numerous other expressions of concern and respect for those who served with him in the British navy. Later, it was Cuthbert Collingwood who sailed into combat alongside Nelson as his second in command at the Battle of Trafalgar.

～

"An Officer desires to return Thanks to Almighty God for his perfect recovery from a severe Wound, and also for the many mercies bestowed upon him."
Written to the minister of St. George's, Hanover Square, London, December 1797

The date of this unsigned note coincides with the recovery of Nelson from the amputation of his arm at the Battle of Santa Cruz. The wound had been painfully slow in healing until the first week of December, when the ligature came away. Within a few days, the arm healed and Nelson was without the debilitating pain and infection that he had suffered from since his return to England from Santa Cruz.

～

"I know their Majesties must feel hurt when they hear these truths. I may be thought presuming, but I trust General Acton will forgive an honest seaman for telling plain truths. As for the other Minister, I do not understand him. We are different men. He has been bred in a Court, and I in a rough element, but I believe my heart is as susceptible of the finer feelings as his, and as compassionate for the distress of those who look up to me for protection."
Written from HMS *Vanguard* off Malta to Sir William Hamilton, Ambassador to the Kingdom of the Two Sicilies, October 1798

Nelson's focus in this relatively long letter was the commitment of the Kingdom of the Two Sicilies to support the Maltese in their resistance to the French. Nelson described his understanding of the responsibility of the King of Naples and asked Sir William to emphasize that responsibility to the kingdom's de facto prime minister, General Sir John Acton. The "other minister" to whom he refers in the letter is the Marquis De Gallo, secretary of state for the Two Sicilies, for whom he held nothing but contempt.

Nelson's case for providing support to the Maltese, who were stubbornly resisting the French, wasn't couched in strategic or tactical terms. His case was based on the obligation to those who were fighting—in this instance under great difficulty—against a common enemy.

~

"I trust, I believe, that your Lordship's goodness of heart, and regard for justice, will recommend Captain Troubridge to His Majesty as equal in merit to any one, on the 1st of August; and I am sure you will add as one of the bravest and very best Sea-Officers in his Service."

Written from Palermo to Earl Spencer, First Sea Lord,
January 1799

Troubridge had the unfortunate luck to run aground as the British fleet sailed into action at the Battle of the Nile, and he was denied the recognition that went to the other British captains at the battle. This letter to the First Sea Lord was part of Nelson's efforts to correct the injustice.

Nelson knew that he had driven his fleet into action very quickly and without adequate charts. What had befallen Troubridge was not due to a lack of seamanship or courage. In fact Troubridge's ship served to mark the outer edge of the shoal that the rest of the fleet successfully cleared on its way to its historic victory at Aboukir Bay. In Nelson's own words, "Captain Troubridge performed the most important service, and was highly instrumental in making the Victory what it was."

There is no doubt that Nelson keenly felt the distress of his brother officer, and he continued his efforts to mitigate Troubridge's desperate disappointment at not having participated in the actual combat in Aboukir Bay. As part of that process, he made strong efforts to counter distant, deskbound questioning of Troubridge's performance.

"[E]very Honour that I receive, it had its origin in your and good Sir Peter's friendship and partiality for me."
Written from Palermo to Margaret Lady Parker, wife of
Admiral Sir Peter Parker, April 1799

Lady Parker and her husband, Admiral Sir Peter Parker, were among Nelson's friends of longest standing. They had met in the West Indies when Nelson was a junior lieutenant and Parker was commander in chief in the theater. There was a genuine affection on their part towards Nelson from the first, and when he was seriously ill during his tour of duty as a lieutenant in the West Indies, he was nursed back to health in their home. When Nelson won his momentous victory at the Battle of the Nile, Lady Parker wrote, "All Europe has cause to bless the day you were born. . . . Sir Peter and I ever regarded you as a Son, and are, of course, truly happy at your well earned Honours."

Although Nelson could, at times, be disdainful of some of his navy's senior leaders, he was capable of forming warm relationships with those he respected. He also did not hesitate to give credit for his successes to mentors who had made genuine contributions to his career.

"Come, then, to your sincere friends. Let us get you well; it will be such a happiness to us all."
Written from Palermo to Earl St. Vincent, June 1799

Earl St. Vincent was among the senior officers with whom Nelson built a strong mentor-pupil relationship. It was as commander in chief at the Battle of Cape St. Vincent in 1797 that Admiral Sir John Jervis earned his title of Earl St. Vincent. And Nelson was a principal architect of the victory. For Nelson's part, he respected St. Vincent's aggressive leadership and the fact that he gave Nelson assignments with the potential for combat. In addition, after Nelson's defeat and the loss of his right arm at the Battle of Santa Cruz, it arguably was Jervis who saved his career.

Nelson's concern over the illness of his friend and senior was no doubt sincere. However, it is safe to assume that going to the royal court of the Kingdom of the Two Sicilies, and having any association with Nelson's controversial relationship with Lady Hamilton there, was the last thing the earl would have wanted to do, sick or healthy.

"You will, in obedience to my orders, prepare everything for the execution of the sentence of the Court-Martial held on John Jolly; but when all the forms, except the last, are gone through, you will acquaint the prisoner, that, although there has been no circumstance to mitigate the severity of the law, yet that I have reason to hope that the sparing of his life will have as beneficial an effect for the discipline of the Service, as if he had suffered death. You will, therefore, respite the prisoner from the sentence of death."
Written from HMS *Foudroyant,* in the Bay of Naples,
to Captain Troubridge, commanding all the British and
Portuguese troops landed from the squadron, July 1799

John Jolly, a marine, had been convicted of the very serious offense of striking an officer. And the sparing of his life did not have "as beneficial effect for the discipline of the Service" as his execution would have had; in all probability, it had a greater effect. Nelson was, without doubt, a strict disciplinarian, but his willingness at times to temper his approach undoubtedly was a factor in the fierce loyalty of the lower decks towards him.

The incident with Jolly occurred at a time when Nelson's professional behavior was subject to much criticism. It was a time of savage retribution against the Neapolitans who had cooperated with the French during the French control of Naples, and Nelson was very much a part of that process. There also was the matter of his unwillingness to leave the proximity of the court of the Kingdom of the Two Sicilies, even to the point of disobeying orders to do so. This apparent fixation on the Two Sicilies was attributed by many to his emotional attachment to Lady Hamilton, who was influential at the Neapolitan court.

The incident with Jolly provided a vivid example of the humane side of Nelson's personality. And simultaneously it showed this sensitivity in sharp contrast with darker aspects of his personality, only one of the provocative contradictions in his character.

"Never mind the Culloden's getting on shore. She has done enough, and I shall write to Lord Spencer by post, that if he does not send you or me another Ship, that your services will be lost for a short time, and even that our Country cannot afford. At all events do not fret yourself."

Written from Palermo to Commodore Sir Thomas
Troubridge, December 1799

Troubridge was one of Nelson's Band of Brothers, and his letter to him reflects empathy for his friend of long standing. He not only is not critical of Troubridge's having gotten his ship "on shore" while landing armament at Malta, but promises to solicit the First Lord of the Admiralty for another ship for him. He kept his promise the next day when he wrote to Earl Spencer, "You will see with some sorrow the accident which has befell the Culloden, and now it only remains for you to decide whether the services of Troubridge are to be lost in the Mediterranean: he must evidently have another Ship, or be an established Commodore."

Nelson's words of encouragement and support in this situation are reminiscent of those he received from his mentor, Earl St. Vincent, after Nelson's crushing defeat at the Battle of Santa Cruz. They are doubly meaningful since Troubridge earlier had gone aground in *Culloden* as he led the British force around unmarked shoals at the beginning of the Battle of the Nile. After that event, Nelson fought hard to gain full battle honors for Troubridge and the crew of *Culloden,* despite the fact that they were never able to free themselves to enter that historic battle.

"I have been long looking for the release of those poor men who were taken by your Cruizers, when carrying provisions to the Island of Malta."
Written from Palermo to the Bey of Tunis, December 1799

It would be easy to take a cynical approach and assume that Nelson's concern for "those poor men" was pro forma in his dealings with the Bey. However, because there were so many other demonstrations of his concern for the ordinary seaman, it can be credited as a reflection of his sincere feelings. What is harder to believe is that Nelson actually believed that the Bey could be persuaded by humanitarian arguments, except perhaps as a means of convincing others of his regal nature.

"I can assure you that one of the greatest rewards in this world is your approbation of my conduct; and in having done my duty in life so fortunately, I have always recollected what pleasure this will give my father."

Written from Palermo to his father, February 1800

Throughout his father's life, Nelson was a dutiful and affectionate son. His father, for his part, expressed pride in his son's accomplishments, and despite the breakup of his son's marriage, he maintained a strong relationship with both his son and Lady Nelson until his death in April 1802.

"The language must be plain, as if flowing from the heart of one of us Sailors who have fought with him."

Written from HMS *San Josef* at Cawsand Bay to Captain Sir Edward Berry, January 1801

When one of the Band of Brothers solicited a contribution for a monument to a brother officer, Captain Ralph Miller, killed in an accidental explosion aboard HMS *Theseus*, Nelson contributed more than money in memory of "poor dear" Miller. He also contributed heartfelt advice about the monument's inscription. Nelson wanted no frippery, simply words that could come from the heart of a fellow sailor. For Nelson, that was higher recognition than flowery phrases. Berry responded with his own plain seaman's eloquence, "[O]ur aim *must be* simplicity. Truth needs no ornaments: Miller requires none, himself was all."

"[T]he moment of a complete victory was surely the proper time to make an opening with the Nation we had been fighting with."

Written from HMS *St. George* to Henry Addington, Prime Minister, May 1801

The Battle of Copenhagen was concluded with a truce initiated by Nelson, an unusual action for a man whose combat doctrine generally included annihilation of the enemy. There were several factors involved. The first was that Nelson considered the Danes to be worthy opponents, which often was not his attitude about the French and particularly the French led by Napoleon. The second was that Nelson knew that he had won the victory and hoped to end the carnage of one of his bloodiest battles. Third, he instinctively knew that leveling Copenhagen and annihilating its defenders would seal long-term Danish enmity for Britain. As it turned out, listening to his heart as well as his battle doctrine not only saved lives but also worked to the strategic advantage of Britain in its struggle against Napoleonic France.

"Respecting poor Maurice's wife, if her necessities require it, every farthing which his kindness gave me shall be used, if she wants it; therefore, I beg you will be everything generous towards her, for she shall ever be by me considered as his honoured wife."
Written from HMS *St. George* in the Bay of Rostock to his friend, Alexander Davison, May 1801

At times referred to as "Poor Blindy," his bachelor brother Maurice's "wife" was actually his mistress, Mrs. Sarah Ford. Despite the informal nature of the relationship between his brother and Sarah, Nelson not only provided financial support for her when Maurice died but also treated her as if she was Maurice's legal wife. There was no condescension in his commitment to assist the blind and penniless woman in her difficult straits.

"I am full of grief for the fate of poor Parker; our only consolation is, that everything has been done which was possible: the breath is not yet gone; but, I dare say, he cannot last until night."
Written from HMS *Amazon* at the Downs to Earl St. Vincent, September 1801

Captain Edward Parker was a Nelson protégé who was fatally wounded in the unsuccessful attack Nelson led on the harbor of Boulogne. After Parker's death from his wound, Nelson, who commanded the attack, said that he thought of him as a son, settled his debts, and paid for his funeral.

"Receive this first letter from your most affectionate Father. If I live, it will be my pride to see you virtuously brought up; but if it pleases God to call me, I trust to Himself: in that case, I have left Lady H. your guardian."
Written from HMS *Victory* off Toulon to
Miss Horatia Nelson Thomson, October 1803

Clearly, Nelson had deep affection for his daughter, Horatia. During the last years of his life, there was considerable evidence in his correspondence of his concern for her well-being and the securing of her future. Horatia married a clergyman and bore nine children. Until her death at age eighty-one, she was convinced that she was Nelson's daughter but denied that Lady Hamilton was her mother.

"I am, therefore, induced from these circumstances to remit the remainder of the said Robert Dwyer's punishment; but I must desire it to be perfectly understood, and to warn the respective Ship's Companies against the commission of crimes of a similar or any other nature, as well as against the shameful disgraceful crime of Desertion, as the sentence of the Court-Martial for either of these offenses, be it death or otherwise, will most certainly be inflicted without mitigation."
Written from HMS *Victory* to all of the captains and
commanders of the ships and vessels on the
Mediterranean station, December 1803

Private Dwyer, a marine, was sentenced to 500 lashes for disobedience to orders and insolence to a superior officer. The mitigation of the sentence by Nelson before the full sentence of 500 lashes was administered almost certainly saved Dwyer's life.

Nelson had taken command of the Mediterranean fleet in May of 1803, and in this message to his captains and commanders, he cited the fact that this was the first offense of such a serious nature that had occurred since his assumption of command. He also cited "the very orderly conduct and good behaviour" of the ships' companies. It is an example of Nelson's approach to punishment, not as an end in itself, but as a means to not only strict discipline but also good morale. It also is an example of the kind of leadership that demonstrated Nelson's sincere concern for the lower decks, and in return, created a powerful personal loyalty towards him.

"Captain Hillyar is most truly deserving of all your Lordship can do for him, and, in addition to his Public merits, has a claim upon us. . . . [A]s the Niger is a very fine fast-sailing Frigate, well-manned, and in most excellent condition, she may be fitted with the Madras's 32 carronades, which are not so heavy as her present nine-pounders, and that your Lordship would recommend her being considered as a Post Ship, either a thirty-two or twenty-eight."

Written from HMS *Victory* to Earl St. Vincent,
First Lord of the Admiralty, January 1804

Nelson's concern for his men was not limited to the lower decks. This intriguing letter demonstrates how Nelson worked to advance the officers who served him well. In the letter, he went beyond the professional qualities of Hillyar, who commanded HMS *Niger,* and also cited his moral qualities. Those attributes had led Hillyar to previously sacrifice a more career-advancing command in order to assure his continued financial support of his mother, sister, and brother. Nelson's appeal to his mentor of many years succeeded, and *Niger* was upgraded to a post ship and Hillyar's career was enhanced.

As a byproduct, the capability of the fleet was improved as well. And in addition to adding insight into Nelson's character, this incident was an example of how, ideally, "loyalty up" is matched by "loyalty down."

∽

"I shall, when I come home, settle four thousand pounds in trustees' hands, for Horatia; for I will not put it in my own power to have her left destitute: for she would want friends, if we left her in this world. She shall be independent of any smiles or frowns."

> Written from HMS *Victory* off Toulon to
> Lady Hamilton, March 1804

The potential vulnerability of an illegitimate girl was indisputable, and Nelson made every effort to create a secure future for his and Lady Hamilton's daughter. As his final tour in the Mediterranean moved towards the history-shaping battle off Cape Trafalgar, Nelson showed increasing concern for Horatia, and took steps to make it clear to her that he was her father.

∽

"I cannot sufficiently thank you for all your kindness to me, and to my dearest friend Lady Hamilton; and thanks is all which I can give you."

> Written from HMS *Victory* to his friend and prize agent,
> Alexander Davison, March 1804

Nelson had met Davison when visiting Quebec in 1782 as captain of HMS *Albermarle.* At that time, Nelson was a young, rising star in the British navy and Davison, ten years older, was a well-off businessman. It was Davison who, soon after they met, dissuaded Nelson from throwing over his naval career for his love of Mary Simpson. In a twist of fate almost twenty years later, it was Davison whom Nelson asked to inform Lady Nelson that he wished no further communication from her.

Davison was among the men who might be considered close friends of Nelson. And the fact that he was supportive of Lady Hamilton when many socially snubbed her was one of the most significant reasons for Nelson's thanks.

"[T]he thought of former days brings all my mother into my heart, which shows itself in my eyes."
> Written from HMS *Victory* off Maddalena Island to
> Dr. Richard Allott, Dean of Raphoe, May 1804

Nelson's mother died when he was nine years old, and this brief letter to the brother of a former rector of Burnham expresses a side of Nelson's personality that sharply contrasted with his ferocity in combat.

"You must, my dear Lord, forgive the warmth I express for Captain Layman; but he is in adversity. . . . If I had been censured every time I have run my Ship, or Fleets under my command, into great danger, I should have long ago been out of the Service, and never in the House of Peers."
> Written from HMS *Victory* to Viscount Melville,
> First Lord of the Admiralty, March 1805

Layman had been censured by a court-martial for running his sloop, HMS *Raven,* aground while performing inshore duty. Earlier in the letter, Nelson pointedly states that carrying out one's duty often requires putting one's ship in harm's way. He also cites the "bravery, zeal, judgment, and activity" of Captain Layman.

This letter is a vivid example of why Nelson inspired exceptional performance from his officers. He realized that a willingness to accept the risks inherent in exercising initiative was an essential quality for his type of naval combat leadership. He encouraged risk taking among his captains, as long as it matched his doctrine, and they rewarded him with both loyalty and the kind of performance required by that doctrine. One of the difficulties associated with Nelson's approach to war fighting was getting understanding from the bureaucratic leadership at the seat of government, a problem that is not unknown to democratic governments to this day.

"I hope to be able to keep Tom at College without one farthing's expense to Mr. Bolton."

Written from HMS *Victory* in Lagos Bay, Portugal, to his sister, Mrs. Thomas Bolton, May 1805

Tom was the eldest son of Nelson's sister, Susanna. And although Nelson was perpetually strapped for money, he made a special effort to provide financial assistance to his family, including the underwriting of the college education of his nephew. In time, Tom Bolton became the second Earl Nelson.

"I was in truth bewildered by the account of Sir Robert Calder's Victory, and the joy of the event; together with the hearing that John Bull was not content, which I am sorry for. Who can, my dear Fremantle, command all the successes which our Country may wish?. . . I should have fought the Enemy, so did my friend Calder; but who can say that he will be more

successful than another? I only wish to stand upon my own merits, and not by comparison, one way or the other, upon the conduct of a Brother Officer."

Written from HMS *Victory* to Captain Thomas Fremantle,
August 1805

Admiral Sir Robert Calder was criticized for not having done more to renew action with Admiral Villeneuve's fleet off Cape Finisterre in July of 1805. The conditions at the time of the action were far from ideal. There was an obscuring mist and Nelson was among those who maintained that Calder had done the best under the circumstances. Nelson also was uncomfortable with the comparisons that were being made between his own aggressiveness and Calder's seeming reticence.

Nelson's attitude was particularly noteworthy since Calder had been vociferously critical of Nelson at the Battle of Cape St. Vincent. There, Calder had complained to their commander in chief, then–Admiral Sir John Jervis, that Nelson had exceeded his orders by breaking out of the line-ahead formation to bring the Spanish force to action. It was an accusation that was rebuffed on the spot by Jervis, who said, "It certainly was so, and if you ever commit such a breach of your orders, I will forgive you also."

Proving that he was not shedding crocodile tears, Nelson ignored the order to send Calder home for his court-martial in a frigate by acceding to Calder's request that he not be "turned out of his own ship," HMS *Prince of Wales.* The ninety-eight-gun *Prince of Wales* was a ship that Nelson could ill afford to spare as the Battle of Trafalgar approached, yet he chose to allow his brother officer to return in that ship with some measure of his stature intact.

"I must beg you will be good enough to recommend James Marguette (Pilot), the bearer hereof . . . to their Lordship's kind attention. He is a most valuable and useful man as a Pilot for

the Leeward Islands, and very handsomely volunteered his services to me . . . and as he is a perfect stranger in London, and consequently will be apt to be imposed upon, I must beg that he may be taken particular care of, and put in a way for a speedy passage to Barbadoes."

Written from HMS *Victory* at Spithead to William Marsden, Secretary of the Admiralty Board, August 1805

Marguette had rendered valuable service to Nelson during his pursuit of Admiral Villeneuve in the West Indies. As circumstances resulted in his being transported to London when Nelson chased Villeneuve back to Europe, Nelson wanted to be sure that Marguette was adequately paid for his services in the West Indies and his time away from his home in Barbados. However, discharging his professional obligation was not enough, and Nelson was notably protective of a man who was in a foreign land, one very different from his own.

~

"Captain . . .'s son is adrift in Italy, at Naples, or Rome; we think, very probably, in prison for debt. His father is very anxious to save the lad. He was Lieutenant of the Hydra and ran away with an opera-dancer from Malta. . . . All we want is to save him from perdition."

Written from HMS *Victory* to Captain Sotheron, HMS *Excellent* at Naples, September 1805

Nelson could be a demanding, sometimes harsh leader. But at other times he demonstrated compassion for weakness in others. In this instance, he was dealing with one of his most hated offenses, desertion. Notwithstanding his attitude about the crime, Nelson had compassion for a fellow officer and tried to assist in finding the young man who presumably had succumbed to the attraction of a female, a circumstance not unknown for naval personnel in foreign theaters.

～

"I am glad Sir Robert Calder is gone; and from my heart I hope he will get home safe, and end his inquiry well."
Letter written from HMS *Victory* to Vice Admiral Cuthbert
Collingwood, October 1805

Calder had been critical of the attention accorded Nelson after the Battle of Cape St. Vincent, and it was Calder who complained to their commander in chief that Nelson had disobeyed a tactical command in the course of his bold maneuver at the beginning of the fighting. However, Nelson repeatedly showed that he did not hold a grudge and was sincerely concerned when Calder, years after the Battle of Cape St. Vincent, was called home to face a court-martial.

Although Nelson often was very critical of other British navy admirals for not being aggressive enough when presented with an opportunity to meet the enemy, he defended Calder's handling of the situation that had precipitated the inquiry. Calder was reprimanded by the court-martial, but continued his career in the British navy until 1815, when he retired. It is interesting to speculate whether or not Nelson's defense of his brother officer tipped the balance against a more serious, career-ending decision by the court.

～

"May the Great God, whom I worship, grant to my Country, and for the benefit of Europe in general, a great and glorious Victory; and may no misconduct in anyone tarnish it; and may human-ity after Victory be the predominant feature in the British Fleet."
The beginning of Nelson's last prayer written aboard
HMS *Victory* shortly before the Battle of Trafalgar,
21 October 1805

Nelson prayed not just for a victory that benefited Britain but for one that benefited all of Europe. He also prayed for humanity to be predominant among the British fleet after the battle, a striking contrast for a leader so committed to annihilating his enemies.

For the hero of the battles of the Nile, Copenhagen, and Trafalgar, an unlikely fusion of combat ferocity and humane sensibility earned him immortality in the hearts of his countrymen. *The Immortality of Nelson;* engraving by Charles Heath, from a painting by Benjamin West.

~

"This day or to-morrow, will be a fortunate one for you, young men."

Attributed by Dr. William Beatty, *Victory*'s surgeon,
as the beginning of the Battle of Trafalgar approached,
21 October 1805

Midshipmen were a regular part of most British navy ship's compliments during Nelson's time. Often they were the sons of relatives or friends of the captain or the embarked flag officer if it was a flagship. It was the beginning point for most naval officers' careers.

Nelson was well known for being both protective and friendly towards the young men who at times were referred to by him as his children. In this comment, made on the quarterdeck of his flagship as it sailed into combat, he was alluding to the fact that participating in a major victory, if they survived, would bring promotions for them.

~

"I leave Emma Lady Hamilton, therefore, a Legacy to my King and Country, that they will give her an ample provision to maintain her rank in life. I also leave to the beneficence of my Country my adopted daughter, Horatia Nelson Thompson; and I desire she will use in future the name of Nelson only. These are the only favors I ask of my King and Country at this moment when I am going to fight their Battle."

From the Codicil to Lord Nelson's will, 21 October 1805

With the French-Spanish Combined Fleet in sight, Nelson's final thoughts before the onslaught of battle were not for himself but for those he loved most. However, the British government never acted on his request on behalf of his paramour and their daughter.

"Love is the wisdom of the fool and
the folly of the wise."
—Dr. Samuel Johnson

10. Fanny and Emma

❦

*"To-day I dine with an English clergyman, a Mr. Andrews,
who has two very beautiful young ladies, daughters. I must
take care of my heart, I assure you."*
Written from St. Omer, France, to his brother,
the Reverend William Nelson, November 1783

Nelson craved affection, and his words to his brother about his
need to take care of his heart struck a prophetic note. His eventual separation from his loyal wife and very public affair with
Lady Hamilton demonstrated how difficult it was for him to
manage his need to love, and be loved.

❦

*"I am just come from Nevis, where I have been visiting Miss
Parry Herbert and a young Widow."*
Written from HMS *Boreas* to his brother the Reverend
William Nelson, May 1785

By the time he first wrote about his future wife, Frances Nisbet, Nelson had already written about being very much in love with at least two other young women, one in Canada, Mary Simpson, and one in France, Elizabeth Andrews.

"My greatest wish is to be reunited with you; and the foundation of all conjugal happiness real love and esteem, is, I trust, what you believe I possess in the strongest degree towards you."
    Written from HMS *Boreas* to his future wife, September 1785

Nelson's initial expressions of love for Fanny suggest that his feelings were based more on a cerebral concept of the institution of marriage than a deeper passion. It also suggests a tendency to create a love for Fanny in his mind that perhaps, notwithstanding his written protestations, did not burn in his heart.

"I open a business which, perhaps, you will smile at, in the first instance, and say, 'This Horatio is forever in love.'... The lady is a Mrs. Nisbet... her personal accomplishments you will suppose I think equal to any person's I ever saw: but, without vanity, her mental accomplishments are superior to most people's of either sex; and we shall come together as two persons most sincerely attached to each other from friendship."
    Written from HMS *Boreas* to his uncle William Suckling,
    November 1785

This description of Fanny was part of a plea for financial assistance from his uncle, who was brother to Maurice Suckling, Nelson's sponsor in the navy. The letter included the statement: "My future happiness, I give you my honour, is now in your power." It was not Nelson's first request for such financial assistance. In January of 1784, he had written a similar letter asking for financial assistance that would put him in a position to marry Elizabeth Andrews, the British clergyman's daughter whom he met in St. Omer, France. As it turned out, Nelson's uncle provided the financial assistance that he requested.

∽

"My heart yearns to you—it is with you; my mind dwells upon nought else but you. Absent from you, I feel no pleasure: it is you, my dearest Fanny, who are everything to me."
Written from HMS *Boreas* to Frances Nisbet, August 1786

One cannot discount the fact that Nelson's loneliness at sea was a significant factor in his love for Fanny. For months at a time he lived with the rigidly regulated sea routine of a British warship. The fatigue, stress, and boredom of such periods, no doubt, were factors in his growing affection for Fanny.

∽

"You have given me a proof that your goodness increases by time. These I trust will ever be my sentiments; if they are not, I do verily believe it will be my folly that occasions it."
Written from HMS *Boreas* to his future wife, February 1787

"Folly" was an interesting choice of a word for Nelson to use to describe any circumstance that would alienate him from his future wife. Years later, when he seemingly had everything a career naval officer could want in terms of success as a combat leader, he jeopardized it all with a notorious love affair with Emma Lady Hamilton.

His recognition of the goodness of his future wife, and his statement that she could not be blamed if his sentiments ever changed, were an indication that he was not overly inclined towards guile. This characteristic was to come to the fore in Nelson's behavior when he fell in love with Lady Hamilton.

"Lady Hamilton has been wonderfully kind and good to Josiah. She is a young woman of amiable manners, and who does honour to the station to which she is raised."
Written from Naples to his wife, September 1793

Nelson made a powerful impression at his first meeting with Sir William Hamilton, who described him to his wife as one "who would become the greatest man that ever England produced." The introduction of Nelson to Lady Hamilton that followed shortly after the meeting with Sir William was the beginning of one of the most controversial aspects of Nelson's life, and one of the most notorious romances of modern history. One wonders if the seemingly offhand comment in Nelson's letter to his wife triggered any sense of alarm on her part.

"I long to hear from you, for a post has arrived without a letter."
Written from a British encampment at Calvi, Corsica, to his wife, July 1794

It's easy to forget that legendary heroes have a human and at times vulnerable side. And like any military person, Nelson longed to hear from home and his wife. In this letter he also writes positively about the activity of his assignment—"I am in all my glory"—and with resignation at his lack of political influence at the Admiralty, "[M]y poor services will not be noticed." It was a letter that could have been written by a million other naval officers in any period of military history.

"I rejoice that my conduct gives you pleasure, and I trust I shall never do anything which will bring a blush on your face, or on that of any of my friends. . . . I trust the time will

come when I may be rewarded, though really I don't flatter myself it is near."

Written from HMS *Agamemnon* at Fiorenzo, Corsica, to his wife, January 1795

Approbation was essential psychic nourishment for Nelson, and Fanny's praise was important to him. The fact that it was dampened by her concerns for his safety and domestic matters probably disappointed him. Notwithstanding his pessimism about being rewarded for his above average performance as a naval officer, a rising tide of public recognition and official honors was to begin in a few years with the Battle of Cape St. Vincent.

"I am so confident of your affection, that I feel the pleasure you will receive will be equal, whether my letter is wrote by my right hand or left . . . and I know that it will add much to your pleasure in finding that Josiah . . . was principally instrumental in saving my life."

Written from HMS *Theseus* to his wife, August 1797

As a considerate husband, Nelson made light of the loss of his arm at the Battle of Santa Cruz. He tried to soften the impact of his wound on his wife by accurately pointing out that it was Josiah, her son by her first marriage, who got him back to his ship and thereby surely saved his life.

One of the sadder aspects of the marriage for Nelson's wife was that the relationship between Nelson and Josiah eventually deteriorated, and over time, Josiah threw away a promising career in the British navy. In October of 1799, Nelson wrote to a fellow admiral, "Perhaps you may be able to make something of Captain Nisbet; he has by his conduct almost broke my heart." Many thought the cause of Josiah's bad behavior was his first-hand observation of the increasingly public love affair between his stepfather and Lady Hamilton. However, Josiah did eventually pursue a successful career in business.

"I have looked over my linen, and find it very different to your list in the articles as follows. . . ."
Written from St. Helens to his wife, April 1798

Nelson's shift in attitude towards his wife after his return to duty in 1798 was clearly discernible in his correspondence to her. In fact, at this point, there was a series of letters in which Nelson complained to Fanny about how his clothing and personal items had been packed. Expressions of his enduring affection were replaced by pointed complaints about mundane matters. The lack of ardor in their marriage that had developed created a receptive environment for the passionate relationship between Nelson and Lady Hamilton that was to come.

"I hope some day to have the pleasure of introducing you to Lady Hamilton, she is one of the very best women in this world; she is an honour to her sex."
Written from Naples to his wife, September 1798

Although he was wise in the ways of the sea and combat, Nelson's lavish praise of Lady Hamilton demonstrated a considerable lack of understanding of the ways of marriage. One can only imagine the reaction of Fanny on reading her husband's description of the woman who was nursing him back to health in Naples, while also heaping ego-enhancing praise on her husband, the newly acclaimed "Hero of the Nile."

Fanny surely must have sensed the contrast between the pampering and praise of Lady Hamilton, and her own restrained recognition of her husband's exploits, which frequently were laced with complaints about his risking his personal safety. And all of her anxiety would be compounded by the fact that Nelson and Lady Hamilton were in a far, distant land.

❧

"The preparations of Lady Hamilton, for celebrating my birth-day to-morrow, are enough to fill me with vanity."
Written from Naples to Lady Nelson, September 1798

Nelson's need for ego enhancement was matched by Lady Hamilton's eagerness to praise him for his spectacularly momentous victory at the Battle of the Nile. That combination of his need for approbation and her constant and lavish praise was to remain an important, perhaps the most important, part of their relationship until his death.

❧

"It will be my duty to provide for your safety, and with it . . . that of their Sicilian Majesties and Family."
Written from Naples to Lady Hamilton, October 1798

Carrying out this promise was the cause of serious problems for Nelson at the Admiralty. In 1799 he ignored orders from Admiral Lord Keith, claiming that his primary mission was to protect the royal family of the Kingdom of the Two Sicilies. The fact that this coincidentally kept Nelson close to Lady Hamilton was not lost on his superiors. They assumed that Nelson was being unduly influenced by his relationship with her.

❧

"I am writing opposite Lady Hamilton, therefore you will not be surprised at the glorious jumble of this letter. Was your Lordship in my place, I much doubt if you could write so well; our hearts and our hands must be all in a flutter: Naples is a dangerous place, and we must keep clear of it."
Written from Naples to Admiral Earl St. Vincent,
October 1798

Fortunately Earl St. Vincent had a very firm and very positive opinion of Nelson as a combat leader. Even this embarrassing outburst did not change that basic opinion.

"You, my dear Lord and friend, make great allowances for my defects. My intentions are good: I vouch for no more. I am well,—never better. Lady Hamilton is an Angel. She has honoured me by being my Ambassadress to the Queen: therefore she has my implicit confidence, and is worthy of it."
Written from Naples to Earl St. Vincent, October 1798

Lady Hamilton's influence with the Queen of the Two Sicilies was a powerful diplomatic factor in Britain's favor. Nelson was to unsuccessfully argue right up to his death that she deserved public recognition and a pension for her service to her country.

"Lady Hamilton's goodness forces me out at noon for an hour. What can I say of hers and Sir William's attention to me? They are, in fact, with the exception of you and my good father, the dearest friends I have in this world."
Written from Naples to his wife, December 1798

Friendship was an important factor in Nelson's relationship with Lady Hamilton, and her husband Sir William Hamilton, British Ambassador to the Kingdom of the Two Sicilies. Sir William was considerably older than his wife, whom he met as Emma Hart when she was his nephew's mistress. And he no doubt was aware of her questionable reputation prior to the relationship with his nephew.[1] Nelson's relationships as friend to Sir William and lover to Lady Hamilton—he referred to the group as the "Tria juncta in uno"—although quite agreeable to the three principals, was the subject of both criticism and ridicule. It also had to be a source of immeasurable anguish for Nelson's wife.

"The whole correspondence relative to this important business was carried out with the greatest address by Lady Hamilton and the Queen, who being constantly in the habits of correspondence, no one could suspect."

Written from Palermo to Admiral Earl St. Vincent, December 1798

Lady Hamilton's close relationship with the Queen of the Kingdom of the Two Sicilies was a great assistance to Nelson. And it added a special dimension to their relationship, making them career helpmates, as well as soulmates.

"To tell you how dreary and uncomfortable the Vanguard appears, is only telling you what it is to go from the pleasantest society to a solitary cell; or, from the dearest friends to no friends."

Written from HMS *Vanguard* to Lady Hamilton, May 1799

At this point, the sailor's loneliness expressed by Nelson relates to Emma, rather than to his wife.

"I received your kind and friendly letter . . . which gave equal pleasure to Sir William, Lady Hamilton, and myself. We are the real Tria juncta in uno."

Written from Palermo to Lord Minto, October 1799

Lord Minto was a friend, one of Nelson's strongest supporters, and the object of extended correspondence with him over the years. Nelson's reference to "three joined in one" was a variation of an earlier reference meant to describe Sir William and Lady Hamilton and Lady Nelson who were joined in their love and admiration for Nelson.

⤳

"I know you are so true and loyal an Englishwoman, that you would hate those who would not stand forth in defence of our King, Laws, Religion, and all that is dear to us. It is your sex that makes us go forth; and seem to tell us—'None but the brave deserve the fair!'"
    Written from HMS *San Josef* to Lady Hamilton, February 1801

Chivalry, patriotism, and romantic love were all part of this statement of love for Lady Hamilton made only weeks before the Battle of Copenhagen. It was written at a time shortly after Nelson finally had separated from his wife. It also was a time that closely followed the deaths of his uncle and benefactor, William Suckling, and William Locker, a professional role model for Nelson as a young officer. Additionally, friendships, such as that with Captain Thomas Troubridge, were being strained by the affair with Lady Hamilton. Based on the circumstances, it had to be a time of emotional difficulty for Nelson.

⤳

"A heart susceptible, sincere, and true;
  A heart, by fate, and nature, torn in two:
One half, to duty and his country due;
  The other, better half, to love and you!"
              Written from HMS *San Josef* to Lady Hamilton,
                             February 1801

One of the most interesting facets of Nelson's personality was the coexistence of extreme romantic sentimentality with the ability coolly to administer mass death and destruction in combat.

⤳

"You will, at a proper time, and before my arrival in England, signify to Lady N. that I expect, and for which I have made such

*a very liberal allowance to her, to be left to myself, and with-
out any inquiries from her; for sooner than live the unhappy life
I did when last I came to England, I would stay abroad for ever.
My mind is fixed as fate: therefore you will send my determination in any way you may judge proper."*

Written from HMS *St. George* to his friend,
Alexander Davison, April 1801

Nelson left it to his friend, Alexander Davison, to finalize his
separation from his wife. His reference to his "unhappy life"
leaves many blanks about what passed privately between husband and wife during the final period of their relationship.
However, one thing was evident. The root of the discord was
Nelson's public affair with Lady Hamilton. And notwithstanding Fanny's remarkably restrained public reaction to the embarrassment of the situation, it finally fractured the marriage.

The family lawyer reported a defining event at the couple's
home at Roundwood, when Lady Nelson's anger erupted.
Increasingly and understandably angered by Nelson's constant
and lavish praise of Lady Hamilton in her presence, she
exclaimed, "I am sick of hearing of dear Lady Hamilton and am
resolved that you shall give up either her or me." Nelson chose
to give up his wife.

Lady Nelson, however, remained loyal up to and after Nelson's death at Cape Trafalgar. On at least one occasion, she
wrote to him seeking a reconciliation. Her letter to Nelson,
written in December of 1801, was simple, nonaccusatory, and
eloquent. She wrote in part: "Do my dear husband, let us live
together. . . . I assure you again I have but one wish in the world,
to please you. Let everything be buried in oblivion, it will pass
away like a dream." The letter was returned marked "Opened by
mistake by Lord Nelson, but not read." The marriage was dead;
Nelson had delivered the death stroke.

〜

*"I send you copies of the King and Queen's letters. I am vexed
that she did not mention you!"*
　　　Written from HMS *Amphion* to Lady Hamilton, July 1803

Lady Hamilton's past, and her publicly displayed status as Nelson's paramour, resulted in frequent social snubbing, both for her
and her lover. Nelson saw only her good qualities, including her
effectiveness on behalf of the British while her husband was
ambassador to the court of the Kingdom of the Two Sicilies.
Naively, he expected her to be treated as a national heroine.
Whatever the rewards of their love, he paid a high price at the
Admiralty, Whitehall, and in British society.

〜

*"Hardy is now busy, hanging up your and Horatia's picture;
and I trust soon to see the other two safe arrived . . . . I want
no others to ornament my cabin."*
　　　Written from HMS *Victory* to Lady Hamilton, August 1803

Lady Hamilton and their illegitimate daughter, Horatia, brought
out the heavily sentimental side of Nelson. As fierce as he was in
combat, he was lavishly affectionate—many felt embarrassingly
so—towards his paramour and their child.

〜

*"Nelson's Alpha and Omega is Emma! . . . I feel that you are
the real friend of my bosom, and dearer to me than life; and
that I am the same to you."*
　　　Written from HMS *Victory* to Lady Hamilton, August 1803

Ten years had elapsed since Nelson's initial meeting with Lady
Hamilton, and at this point she was firmly established as the
object of the love and ego enhancement he craved.

"I shall endeavour to do what is right, in every situation; and some ball may soon close all my accounts with this world of care and vexation!"
Written from HMS *Victory* to Lady Hamilton, October 1803

During the years after his victories at the Nile and Copenhagen, Nelson was the target of innumerable requests. Many of the requests to use his presumed influence at the Admiralty on behalf of both individuals and causes were directed through Lady Hamilton, who had become an integral part of his public life. Although his responses to the requests were often accompanied by disclaimers that he had little influence at the seat of British naval power, he invariably did his best to help those who sought his intervention on their behalf.

Many of Nelson's letters leading up to the Battle of Trafalgar vent his frustration and weariness to Lady Hamilton, now his closest confidante. Nelson's reference to "some ball" that would "close all my accounts" was prescient and represented inner thoughts shared with his paramour. Two years after this letter, a musket ball fired by a French sharpshooter at the Battle of Trafalgar, although considerably smaller than the type of cannon shot to which he surely referred in his letter, ended his life.

"I have left you a part of the rental of Bronte. . . . It is but common justice; and, whether Mr. Addington gives you anything, or not, you will want it."
Written from HMS *Victory* to Lady Hamilton, March 1804

The well-being of Lady Hamilton after his death was an ongoing concern for Nelson. He unsuccessfully solicited Whitehall to provide a pension to Lady Hamilton for her significant, but unofficial, efforts while her husband served as ambassador of the

Kingdom of the Two Sicilies. The income from Bronte, the estate attached to the dukedom given to Nelson by the King of the Kingdom of the Two Sicilies after the Battle of the Nile, was not substantial. This concern for the future security of Lady Hamilton was prominent in many of Nelson's last letters, written just hours before the Battle of Trafalgar. His concern for her future welfare was well-founded. After his death, dwindling friendships, an excessive lifestyle, and heavy drinking led to a tragic end for her.

"You will readily fancy all I would say, and do think."
Written from HMS *Victory* to Lady Hamilton, April 1804

Nelson's belief that Lady Hamilton would know his thoughts demonstrates that he considered her to be his soulmate.

"But, from us, what can they find out? That I love you most dearly; and hate the French most damnably."
Written from HMS *Victory* to Lady Hamilton, May 1804

A cutter carrying personal letters from Lady Hamilton to Nelson was captured by the French. Although the potential for embarrassment was present, the occasion demonstrated Nelson's attitude that his relationship with Lady Hamilton, although outside conventional social standards, was not something to hide. In fact, after he separated from Lady Nelson he occasionally refers to Lady Hamilton as his wife in his letters to her.

"Do not believe a syllable the newspapers say, or what you hear. Mankind seems fond of telling lies."
Written from HMS *Victory* to Lady Hamilton, May 1804

Although much of Nelson's status as a hero was based on lauda-
tory descriptions of his combat feats in the newspapers of the
time, those newspapers were less kind in their treatment of his
personal life. Cartoons ridiculing his extramarital relationship
were particularly cutting.

❧

*"You will not hear of my making Prize–money. I have not
paid my expenses these last nine months."*
Written from HMS *Victory* to Lady Hamilton, July 1804

Although many naval officers accumulated considerable fortunes
from their prize money, Nelson, notwithstanding his combat successes, never became rich. He was generous towards relatives in
need and, like most British navy senior officers, he had many
expenses for which he was not reimbursed. In addition, the purchase and improvements of Merton, the comfortable but far from
luxurious home he secured for himself and Lady Hamilton,
stretched his finances.

❧

*"Brave Emma! good Emma! If there were more Emmas, there
would be more Nelsons; you have penetrated my thoughts."*
Attributed by Captain Henry Blackwood during a visit to
Merton, September 1805

Blackwood visited Nelson when he was on leave at Merton
shortly before the Battle of Trafalgar. During their discussion,
Lady Hamilton reacted to a statement by Nelson that he "was as
happy as possible" at Merton. She pointed out that what he really
wanted to do was to get at the French and Spanish fleets, which
he considered to be "his own property." Nelson's response to her
insight was another of his well-turned phrases that has taken on
its own life in literature. It should be noted that this incident was
reported in an 1806 biography of Nelson which was heavily influenced by Lady Hamilton.

~

"I intreat, my dear Emma, that you will cheer up; and we will look forward to many, many happy years, and be surrounded by our children's children. God Almighty can, when he pleases, remove the impediment. My heart and soul is with you and Horatia."

Written from HMS *Victory* to Lady Hamilton,
September 1805

These words of comfort, after a brief respite with Lady Hamilton and Horatia at Merton, take on a painful poignancy in the face of Nelson's death at Trafalgar only a month later. The "impediment" presumably was his wife, who despite the harsh rejection by her husband and the public embarrassment of the relationship between her husband and Lady Hamilton, remained steadfastly loyal to Nelson throughout his and her lives.[2]

~

"Receive, my dearest Horatia, the affectionate parental blessing of your Father."

Written from HMS *Victory* to Horatia Nelson, October 1805

With thinly veiled pretenses, and to varying degrees, Nelson and Lady Hamilton masked the fact that Horatia was their child. However, on the eve of mortal combat, all pretenses were blown away, and Nelson ended his last letter to his daughter unequivocally and simply as "your Father."

~

"I leave Emma Lady Hamilton, therefore, a Legacy to my King and Country, that they will give her an ample provision to maintain her rank in life."

Codicil to Nelson's will written aboard HMS *Victory,*
October 1805

No provision, ample or otherwise, was provided for Lady Hamilton by her king or country. Although her husband and Nelson provided a modest income for her after their deaths, she died a pauper in France in 1815, a victim of her grief, extravagant spending, and excessive drinking.[3]

"My dearest beloved Emma, the dear friend of my bosom. . . . May the God of Battles crown my endeavours with success; at all events, I will take care that my name shall ever be most dear to you and Horatia, both of whom I love as much as my own life. And as my last writing before the Battle will be to you, so I hope in God that I shall live to finish my letter after the Battle."
Written from HMS *Victory* to Lady Hamilton,
19 October 1805

There was to be no finish to the letter after the Battle of Trafalgar.

> "The purest treasure mortal times afford
> Is spotless reputation; that away,
> Men are but gilded loam or painted clay."
> —Shakespeare

11. Reputation

"The character of an Officer is his greatest treasure: to lower that, is to wound him irreparably."

> Written from HMS *Boreas* at Basseterre, St. Kitts, to Thomas Lord Sydney, British Secretary of State, March 1785

Even at a young age—he was not yet thirty years old—Nelson was mindful of his reputation. In this instance, he was defending himself against complaints from the merchants of St. Kitts and Nevis about his strict enforcement of Britain's Navigation Acts. Although he placed great importance on preserving his reputation, he chose performing his duty, as he saw it, over the risk of official sanctions. His position was eventually upheld by the Admiralty, reinforcing his commitment to relying on his own interpretation of his duty, no matter what the political risk.

"Whatever may be my fate, I have no doubt in my own mind but that my conduct will be such, as will not bring a blush on

the face of my friends: the lives of all are in the hands of Him,
who knows best whether to preserve mine or not; to His will
I do resign myself. My character and good name are in my own
keeping. Life with disgrace is dreadful. A glorious death is to
be envied; and if anything happens to me, recollect that death
is a debt we must all pay, and whether now, or in a few years
hence, can be of little consequence."

Written from HMS *Agamemnon* to his wife, March 1795

This remarkable summary of Nelson's state of mind as he
approached a battle with the French fleet puts the initial emphasis on assuring his reputation. As it turned out, the battle was,
in Nelson's later words, only a "brush" with the enemy. At this
point, all of Nelson's hero-building fleet engagements were still
to come. But in a matter of two years, at the Battle of Cape St.
Vincent, his "character and good name" would become public
property and no longer a matter only for his own keeping. The
statement that "a glorious death is to be envied" was, in light of
the Battle of Trafalgar, which was still ten years in the future,
prophetic. Doubtless, this letter was a sincere effort by Nelson
to reassure his wife. Given what now is known of Fanny's personality, it probably had the opposite effect.

"[O]ne Captain told me, 'You did just as you pleased in Lord
Hood's time, the same in Admiral Hotham's, and now again
with Sir John Jervis; it makes no difference to you who is Com-
mander-in-Chief.' I returned a pretty strong answer to this
speech."

Written from HMS *Agamemnon* in the Gulf of Genoa
to his wife, January 1796

By early 1796, Nelson had earned a reputation within the British
navy as an aggressive leader. He also had demonstrated a

propensity for acting on his own initiative, at times in contra-
diction to his orders. Inevitably, there was envy towards him
among some of his fellow officers. There also was an understandable concern that his highly visible departures from orders
would compromise good order and discipline within the British
navy. As concerned as Nelson was with his reputation, it is noteworthy that he was willing to risk the criticism of others, even
risk his career, to pursue what he saw as the greater objectives of
his missions.

In a letter to Lady Nelson three days prior to this one, he
proudly described how much confidence his commander in
chief, Admiral Sir John Jervis, placed in him. Revealing how he
hoped his growing reputation would please his wife, he wrote,
"The credit I derive from all these compliments must be satisfactory to you." Lady Nelson's inability to empathize with Nelson's feelings about his career was to contribute to the demise of
their relationship.

≈

*"He seems at present to consider me more as an associate than
a subordinate Officer; for I am acting without any orders."*
Written from HMS *Agamemnon* off the Hieres Islands
to his wife, February 1796

The very visible trust that Admiral Jervis showed in Nelson was
clear recognition of Nelson's growing reputation as a rising officer. That recognition was both psychologically nourishing to
Nelson's considerable ego and a powerful reinforcement for his
willingness to take politically risky initiatives.

≈

*"A person sent me a letter, and directed as follows. 'Horatio
Nelson, Genoa.' On being asked how he could direct in such
a manner, his answer, in a large party, was, 'Sir, there is but*

*one Horatio Nelson in the world.' . . . I am known through-
out Italy; not a Kingdom, or State, where my name will be
forgotten. This is my Gazette."*

Written from HMS Captain to his wife, August 1796

Nelson's pride in his reputation was well earned; he had been a
most active and successful captain in the Mediterranean for
three years. This passage suggests an effort to impress Lady Nelson with his professional stature. A later passage suggests that
Lady Nelson was not showing an appropriate—at least in Nelson's view—appreciation of his accomplishments at this point
in his career. It read, "You ask me when I shall come home? I
believe, when either an honorable peace is made, or a Spanish
war, which may draw our fleet out of the Mediterranean."

*"I send you a short Detail of the transactions of the Captain;
and if you approve of it, are at perfect liberty to insert in the
newspapers. . . . As I do not write for the press, there may be
parts of it which require the pruning-knife, which I desire you
will use without fear."*

Written from HMS Irresistible in Lagos Bay to his friend,
Captain William Locker, Lieutenant-Governor of the
Greenwich Naval Hospital, February 1797

Immediately after the Battle of Cape St. Vincent, Nelson wrote
a series of letters to friends and relatives that were, notwithstanding his statement about not writing for the press, clearly
intended for publication. To some extent, this bit of letter writing was precipitated by Nelson's belief that his commander in
chief at the time, Admiral Sir John Jervis, did not give him sufficient credit for the victory in his official dispatches. In addition there were those, like then–Captain Robert Calder, who
believed that Nelson's action of leaving the British line-ahead

formation at the beginning of the battle was a violation of the British navy's Fighting Instructions and the commander in chief's signals. Whether or not Jervis had unfairly underplayed Nelson's role, or simply played fair with all of those who honorably participated in the battle, Nelson embarked on an effort to make his achievements at Cape St. Vincent widely known in Britain.

Nelson's personal public relations campaign succeeded, perhaps beyond his expectations. As a result of the Battle, which was a desperately needed victory for Britain, Nelson was catapulted to national fame. His reputation as a warrior dramatically grew up to his death at the Battle of Trafalgar; it continues unabated after two centuries.

"'Nelson's patent Bridge for boarding First-rates' will be a saying never forgotten in this Fleet, where all do me the justice that I deserve. The Victory, and every Ship in the Fleet, passing the glorious group, gave me three cheers."
Written from HMS *Irresistible* off Lagos Bay to his uncle
William Suckling, February 1797

The letter containing these lines was written only a few days after Nelson's detailed report of his exploits sent to Captain Locker. The term "Nelson's patent Bridge for boarding First-rates" described Nelson's use of one conquered Spanish ship to cross over with a boarding party from his flagship to a second Spanish ship of the line. The three ships had come together during the Battle of Cape St. Vincent.

The bold action by Nelson was a vivid example of his ability to seize opportunities as they occurred during battle. His passing along of the phrase was an example of his ability to create a memorable saying to dramatize his exploits. Over two centuries, the colorful phrase has become deeply embedded in Nelson lore.

Nelson's career-risking initiative and fearlessness in leading boarding parties at the Battle of Cape St. Vincent rocketed him to public fame in Britain. *The San Nicolas and San Joseph Carried by Boarding, February 14, 1797;* engraving by R. Golding, from a painting by Richard Westall.

⌒

*"A few nights ago a Paper was dropped on the quarter deck, of
which this is a copy:—'Success attend Admiral Nelson! God
bless Captain Miller! We thank them for the Officers they have
placed over us. We are happy and comfortable, and will shed
every drop of blood in our veins to support them, and the name
of the Theseus shall be immortalized as high as the Captain's.'"*
Written from HMS *Theseus* to his wife, June 1797

At this time there was considerable discontent, which had risen
to mutinies at Spithead, the Nore, and elsewhere, in the ranks
of the British navy. In the Mediterranean, *Theseus* was among
the ships with dangerously low morale. The fleet's commander
in chief, Admiral Earl St. Vincent, removed her commanding
officer. Captain Ralph Miller was placed in command and Nelson shifted his flag to the troubled ship. Both recently had distinguished themselves at the Battle of Cape St. Vincent, and
their reputations as tough warfighters surely were an important
part of the change of morale among the ship's company.

⌒

*"It is the part of a friend to take care of the reputation of an
absentee: you have performed that part, and have my gratitude
. . . whilst I live, I never shall forget the few real friends I have
in this world—but amongst them, I hope, I may rank you."*
Written from Palermo to Vice Admiral Samuel Goodall,
January 1799

This statement was a response to an earlier letter from Goodall
congratulating Nelson on his victory at the Battle of the Nile.
The earlier letter went far beyond normal congratulations; it
dealt at length with the way Goodall had defended Nelson
against his detractors at home. At one point, Goodall writes of
how "I have often been obliged to stand in the breach against

the senseless criticisms of the noble and ignoble of this Country; you know them well-governed by the tide of sure and immediate success."

Nelson did indeed know them well. In fact, during his hunt for Napoleon's invasion fleet that led up to the Battle of the Nile, there had been criticism of him for not being able to find so large a force as that of the French fleet headed for Egypt. And subsequently, there was significant criticism of him as he increasingly appeared to be influenced, managed according to many, by Lady Hamilton after the Battle of the Nile. Finally, Nelson's commander in chief, Admiral Lord Keith, who referred to the situation at the court of the Two Sicilies as "a scene of fulsome vanity and absurdity," and his supporters at the Admiralty and Whitehall combined to precipitate his return to England.

"The high compliments you are paying me are far, very far beyond my deserts. Believe me, my dear friend, my only wish is to sink with honour into my grave, and when that shall please God, I shall meet death with a smile—not that I am insensible to the honours and riches my King and Country have heaped upon me, so much more than any Officer can deserve, yet I am ready to quit this world of trouble; and envy none, but those of the estate six feet by two. God knows when I may see England. I cannot quit my post with honour."

Written from Palermo to his friend, Alexander Davison,
February 1799

This letter to Davison was an example of how, at times, Nelson recorded his innermost thoughts in his correspondence. By this time he was a battle-scarred national hero, and despite his romance with Lady Hamilton, his own particular version of combat fatigue had begun to show through. As a result, his drive for honor and reputation began to take on a more philosophical perspective. But despite this flash of morbidness, he went on to still greater fame in two additional history-making battles for Britain at Copenhagen and Cape Trafalgar and to father a daughter whom he deeply loved.

∿

"One day or other I shall rest from all my labours. I still find it good to serve near home, there a man's fag and services are easily seen; next to that, is writing a famous account of your own actions."

Written from Palermo to his wife, November 1799

Notwithstanding Nelson's comments to his wife, his notewor- thy naval service, including his legend-making actions at the battles of Cape St. Vincent, the Nile, Copenhagen, and Trafal- gar, was not fought near home. On the other hand, his opinion about self-promotion was, in his own case, extremely accurate.

∿

"I shall send it to the Board of Admiralty, that they may either support the dignity of the Admiral they have entrusted with the command of the Mediterranean fleet, or remove him."

Written from Palermo to Charles Lock,
British Consul at Naples, December 1799

The "it" in this passage was a letter from Lock to Nelson. The letter in question was part of an exchange of correspondence among Lock, Nelson, and the Admiralty about provisioning British navy ships in the Mediterranean. Lock was no friend of Nelson, or for that matter, of the Hamiltons. Nelson believed, probably with justification, that Lock actively was attempting to undermine him at home. However, Nelson obviously also believed that his reputation in Britain was such at this time that it would carry the day in any dispute with a junior, local British diplomat. After a meeting between the two, Nelson wrote a letter to the Admiralty Board withdrawing a demand he had made for an inquiry. The reason, he stated, was to not cause "the ruin of Mr. Lock's character."

"I have regretted sincerely the escape of Buonaparte; but those ships which were destined for me for the two places where he would certainly have been intercepted, were . . . obliged to be at Malta . . . therefore, no blame lays at my door."
Written from Palermo to Lord Elgin, British Ambassador in Constantinople, December 1799

Napoleon's escape back to France from his stranded army in Egypt was, in some ways, more serious than his evasion of the British navy on his way to Egypt in the first place. Although Napoleon had successes in his campaign in Egypt, Nelson's victory at the Battle of the Nile caused his military expedition there eventually to collapse. On the other hand, when Napoleon succeeded in getting back to France after the failed thrust towards the Far East, he embarked on new military campaigns that cost many thousands of lives in Europe. In the process, he managed for many more years to grievously threaten Britain's security.

Nelson did not want to be blamed for Napoleon's escape from Egypt. And although there were some who would have liked to do so, his forces were spread too thinly and occupied too intensively for him to be expected realistically to cover Napoleon's escape back to France. In addition, Nelson's reputation was too firmly established by that time to be seriously shaken.

"[I]t has been my extraordinary good fortune to capture the Généreux, 74, bearing the Flag of Rear-Admiral Perrée, and a very large Storeship, with 2000 troops and provisions and

stores for the relief of La Valette. . . . [T]his, my dear Lord,
makes nineteen Sail of the Line and four Admirals I have been
present at the capture of, this war."

Written from HMS *Foudroyant* off Malta to his friend,
Lord Minto, February 1800

In his personal correspondence, particularly that with friends
with political power, Nelson very frequently wrote with his reputation in mind.

❧

"The Lady of the Admiralty never had any just cause for being
cool to me. Either as a public or private [man], I wish noth-
ing undone which I have done."

Written from HMS *San Josef* to his friend,
Alexander Davison, January 1801

"The Lady of the Admiralty" could have been the astute wife of
the First Lord of the Admiralty, Lord Spencer. She also could
have been the domineering wife of Evan Nepean, Secretary to
the Admiralty.

By early 1801, Nelson had separated from his wife and was
frequently appearing in public with Lady Hamilton. After his
harsh dismissal of his wife, the open romance with Lady Hamilton frequently was not well received by London officialdom or
in social circles. By this time, Nelson saw Lady Hamilton as his
"wife" in all respects, lacking only the formality of a marriage
ceremony. Others saw the relationship differently and Nelson's
personal reputation suffered accordingly.

❧

"As both my friends and enemies seem not to know why I sent
on shore a Flag of Truce—the former, many of them, thought
it was a ruse de guerre, and not quite justifiable; the latter, I

believe, attributed it to a desire to have no more fighting, and a few, very few, to the cause that I felt, and which I trust in God I shall retain to the last moment, humanity."

Written from HMS *St. George* in the Baltic to
Henry Addington, Prime Minister, May 1801

Despite his many protestations to the contrary, Nelson was constantly concerned about his reputation. After the Battle of Copenhagen, there were those who criticized his offering of a truce to the Danes before they were completely crushed. This letter to his prime minister was a detailed explanation that showed an extremely humane, perceptive, and strategically sound rationale for the offering of the truce at the "moment of a complete victory." After making his case Nelson ended with convincing emphasis, saying simply, "I wish my reputation to stand upon its merits."

"I dare say, Monsieur La Touche will have a different sort of letter to write, if I can once get a shake at him. Whether the world thinks that I ran away or no, is to me a matter of great indifference. If my character is not fixed by this time, it is useless for me to try to fix it at my time of life."

Written from HMS *Victory* to his friend,
Alexander Davison, August 1804

Ten days before this letter to Davison, Nelson reported to the Admiralty that Admiral La Touche-Tréville had "cut a caper a few miles outside of Toulon." Although the French squadron never sailed beyond the cover of the batteries protecting Toulon, and quickly returned to port, La Touche-Tréville wrote in a report to Paris that he had pursued Nelson as Nelson fled before him. Nelson, showing that it was not a matter of indifference, made sure that he protected his reputation by putting the lie to the claim in both his official and private correspondence. He also threatened to make La Touche-Tréville eat his message if he ever caught up to him in combat. As it turned out, La Touche-Tréville and Nelson never met in combat; the French admiral died shortly after his "caper." It was Admiral Villeneuve who led the French-Spanish Combined Fleet that Nelson crushed a little more than a year later at Cape Trafalgar.

"Indeed, we all draw so well together in the Fleet, that I flatter myself the sorrow for my departure will be pretty general."
Written from HMS *Victory* to Lady Hamilton,
September 1804

As Nelson anticipated leave from the Mediterranean fleet, his reputation at all levels among the ships had become an independent force. After a brief leave, he returned, and that force was a significant factor in his electrifying victory at the Battle of Trafalgar on 21 October 1805.

"But for General Brereton's dammed information, Nelson would have been, living or dead, the greatest man in his Profession that England ever saw. Now, alas! I am nothing—perhaps shall incur censure for misfortunes which may happen, and have happened."
Written from HMS *Victory* to his friend,
Alexander Davison, July 1805

During Nelson's pursuit of Admiral Villeneuve in the West Indies, erroneous information had caused him to miss a close opportunity for the battle he desperately sought. There was a great deal of political risk in Nelson's decision to pursue Admiral Villeneuve and the French fleet from the Mediterranean to the West Indies. And he knew there could be dire consequences if Villeneuve escaped his grasp to link up with other French units for an invasion of England. Nelson very correctly understood that an admiral's reputation—even his—could turn on a single event. However, in a matter of months, he had his opportunity at Cape Trafalgar, where he did become "the greatest man in his Profession that England ever saw."

"I had their huzzas before—I have their hearts now!"
Attributed by Clarke and M'Arthur, early Nelson biographers, September 1805

Public adulation was one of the principal psychological supports on which Nelson relied during the difficult final years of his career. As he left the Portsmouth landing for *Victory* and immortality at the Battle of Trafalgar, he was cheered loudly by the crowds gathered along the shoreline. His comment to his flag captain, Thomas Hardy, showed that he understood that he had progressed from gratitude for his victories to an emotional public attachment to his person.

"I believe my arrival was most welcome, not only to the Commander of the Fleet, but also to every individual in it; and, when I came to explain to them the 'Nelson touch,' it was like an electric shock. Some shed tears, all approved—'It was new—it was singular—it was simple!'; and, from Admirals downwards, it was repeated—'It must succeed, if ever they will allow us to get at them! You are, my Lord, surrounded by friends whom you inspire with confidence.' Some may be Judas's; but the majority are certainly much pleased with my commanding them."
Written from HMS *Victory* to Lady Hamilton, October 1805

Nelson's relationship with his captains and admirals was symbiotic. Their loyalty supported him; his demeanor and reputation for success in battle inspired them. Intriguingly, Nelson did not actually define the "Nelson touch" in this letter to Lady Hamilton; he simply described its dramatic effect on his audience. For many the term has become a label for his tactical plan for the Battle of Trafalgar, which was included in his detailed memorandum to his captains on 9 October 1805. For others it has come to include his unequaled, but less susceptible to precise analysis, leadership.

In any event, it is indisputable that Nelson's hard-earned combat reputation throughout the British navy was a primary factor in the emotional response to his joining the British fleet in September of 1805, and to the fierce loyalty of those who followed him to his historic victory only weeks later. With his death at Trafalgar, Nelson's reputation passed to the care of others. Today that reputation is immortalized in innumerable books, films, and television programs, as well as at sites like the Royal Naval Museum in Portsmouth and the National Maritime Museum in Greenwich.

"Be absolute for Death; either death or life shall
therefore be the sweeter."
"I hold my duty as I hold my soul."
—Shakespeare

12. Life and Death

~

*"[W]e all rise by deaths. I got my rank by a shot killing a Post-
Captain, and I most sincerely hope I shall, when I go, go out
of the world the same way; then we go all in the line of our
Profession—a Parson praying, a Captain fighting."*
Written from HMS *Albemarle* at Portsmouth to his brother,
the Reverend William Nelson, February 1782

There were hard realities in the British navy of Nelson's time,
and one of the most rigid was that once an officer reached the
rank of post captain he could not advance up the promotion list
except by the death or retirement of someone senior to him.
Thus, Nelson's attitude about death was not solely a matter of
philosophy; it also was a pragmatic matter related to his career
advancement. And he indeed did "go" as he hoped, fighting in
the line of his profession at the Battle of Trafalgar.

"[H]ow uncertain are human expectations, and how vain the idea of fixing periods for happiness."

Written from HMS *Boreas* to his future wife,
Frances Nisbet, March 1786

Absence from one's love is an ongoing condition in the life of a seaman. It had to be particularly painful for Nelson, whose emotions were generally very close to the surface of his personality.

"Mankind are not always what they seem."

Written from HMS *Boreas* in Portsmouth to
Prince William Henry, August 1787

There is no doubt that Nelson curried favor with Prince William Henry, but in this surprising letter he presumed to give him some big-brotherly advice about life, and it was undeniably sound advice. Earlier in the letter he admonishes that, "Princes seldom, very seldom, find a disinterested person to communicate their thoughts to." Without doubt, as Nelson advanced to senior ranks in his profession, he inevitably suffered from the same problem—admirals seldom hear the truth—demonstrated in different contexts.

"Not being a man of fortune is a crime which I cannot get over, and therefore none of the Great care about me . . . and now I see the propriety of not having built my hopes on such sandy foundations as the friendships of the Great."

Written from Burnham to his mentor and friend,
Captain William Locker, September 1789

At this time, Nelson was living on half pay and without a navy assignment. It was a testing time, and he was personally experiencing how the Admiralty's decisions about ship assignments were heavily weighted in favor of those with political and social influence. Doubtless, he felt let down by Prince William Henry and others with influence at the Admiralty whom he believed would act on his behalf.

∽

"[G]ood wishes, without something more powerful, are of no avail in this Country."

Written from Burnham to Messers. Wilkinson and Higgins in Antigua, November 1789

Before being brought home and placed on half pay by the British navy, Nelson had attempted to call government attention to official corruption in Britain's West Indian colonies. He had been provided with extensive documentation of fraud by Messers. Wilkinson and Higgins, who were merchants in Antigua, and who expected to be paid a commission on all funds recovered from the resulting investigation. As so often happens in matters of misbehavior in high places, Nelson, as the "messenger" of the incriminating information, came under attack himself.

Despite the fact that some reform and recovery of funds came from the episode, there was little satisfaction for Nelson. In fact, the affair strengthened his growing conviction that, in real life, influence was what counted in the power centers of Whitehall and the Admiralty.

∽

"A glorious death is to be envied; and if anything happens to me, recollect that death is a debt we must all pay, and whether now, or a few years hence, can be of little consequence."

Written from HMS *Agamemnon* to his wife, March 1795

An eighteenth century naval officer faced mortal danger with regularity. The very act of going to sea exposed him to fatal diseases and accidents. And to that was added the prospect, as Nelson's uncle Maurice Suckling put it, "a cannon ball may knock off his head and provide for him at once."

Nelson not only spoke convincingly of how he was reconciled to his death, but he dramatically and repeatedly proved it in combat. And as a corollary to his acceptance of the unpredictability of his end, he accepted his numerous wounds as a normal byproduct of his profession.

"[T]o-morrow my head will probably be crowned with either laurel or cypress."
Written from HMS *Theseus* opposite the town of Santa Cruz, Tenerife, to his commander in chief, Admiral Earl St. Vincent, July 1797

Nelson often saw a mission as a simple choice between glorious victory or death. In his attack of Santa Cruz, neither resulted. The British attack was repulsed with significant casualties among Nelson's force. He himself suffered a serious wound that resulted in the amputation of his right arm. The wound was serious enough to almost end his life, but he survived to go on to earn unprecedented laurels on future occasions.

"[S]oon, very soon, we must all be content with a plantation of six feet by two, and I probably shall possess this estate much sooner than is generally thought."
Written from Palermo to Vice Admiral Goodall, January 1799

The analogy between death and occupying a grave-size "plantation" was one that Nelson used more than once in his writing.

Hand-to-hand combat was among the scores of life-and-death situations faced by Nelson. *Rear Admiral Nelson's Conflict in His Barge with a Spanish Launch, Night of July 3, 1797;* engraving by A. Smith, from a painting by Richard Westall.

❧

"When I go hence, and am no more seen, I shall have very few to regret me. My health is such that without a great alteration, I will venture to say a very short space of time will send me to that bourne from whence none return; but God's will be done."
Written from Palermo to Margaret Lady Parker, wife of Admiral Sir Peter Parker, Nelson's mentor from his days as a young officer, February 1799

In another analogy for death—this one borrowed from Shakespeare's soliloquy "to be or not to be"—Nelson chose a reference to a boundary. His opinion that very few would regret him could not have been more mistaken. His funeral six years later was a national event; he was emotionally mourned by an entire nation, and his fame has maintained astonishing momentum through two turbulent centuries.

❧

"[V]ictories cannot be obtained without blood."
Written from Palermo to Captain Foote, HMS *Seahorse,* June 1799

Just as Nelson was prepared to pay for victory with his own blood, he clearly was not squeamish about casualties in combat.

❧

"If the war goes on, I shall be knocked off by a ball, or killed with chagrin. My conduct is measured by the Admiralty by the narrow rule of law, when I think it should have been done by that of common sense. I restored a faithful Ally by breach of orders—Lord Keith lost a fleet by obedience, against his own sense, yet as one is censured, the other must be approved."
Written from Palermo to his friend, Alexander Davison, August 1799

When one considers the importance Nelson placed on his reputation and honors, this statement loses much of its flippancy. One
of the foundation stones of Nelson's career was his willingness to
disobey an order on the basis of his own real time, on-scene judgment of what would achieve the large objective involved. His
dilemma was one that brilliant military leaders, who are subject
to overriding civilian control, must accommodate.

At the time this letter was written, there was a special factor involved that weighed heavily against and on Nelson. He
had indeed disobeyed Keith's orders so that he might remain
close to the Kingdom of the Two Sicilies, which anchored
Britain's alliances in the Mediterranean. A strong argument can
be made that his decision saved that ally. The special factor was
that his decision to remain close to the Two Sicilies also kept
him close to his paramour, Lady Hamilton. And many felt
strongly that she was wielding undue influence over his actions.

"My only wish is, to do as I would be done by."
Written from HMS *Foudroyant* at Port Mahon to
Rear Admiral Sir John Duckworth, October 1799

In this context, Nelson was writing about a basic rule for divid-
ing prize money, but it was a principle that he also applied to
other aspects of his life. Perhaps the most important exception
was the manner in which he separated from his wife.

*"It is warm work, and this day may be the last to any of us at a
moment; but mark you, I would not be elsewhere for thousands."*
Attributed by then–Colonel William Stewart, an eyewitness
to the Battle of Copenhagen, 2 April 1801

Warm work was a significant understatement for the proceed-
ings of one of the bloodiest naval battles of the era. However, for

Nelson and the others in the British fleet, it was an opportunity for honor and professional advancement. And those inducements outweighed, for many, even the real prospect of death.

～

"My health is gone, and although I should be happy to try and hold out a month or six weeks longer, yet death is no respecter of persons. I own, at present, I should not wish to die a natural death."

> Written from HMS *St. George* to Henry Addington,
> Prime Minister, May 1801

Notwithstanding his writings about the benefits of dying in battle, it is evident that, increasingly, Nelson would have liked to die a natural death at Merton with his beloved Emma. Fate decided that it would be in battle.

～

"As the dead cannot be called back, it is of no use dwelling on those who are gone."

> Written from HMS *St. George* to his friend,
> Alexander Davison, May 1801

This expression of resignation to the death of loved ones was precipitated by the death of Nelson's brother Maurice. Moving quickly from the pragmatic approach to death required in his profession, Nelson turned to the matter of Maurice's mistress, who was blind, crippled, and penniless. He expressed his concern clearly: "I am sure you will do everything which is right for his poor blind wife." He insisted on treating Maurice's mistress as if the couple were married, and Nelson himself provided for her financial support with an annuity that lasted until she died approximately ten years later. This event demonstrated that although Nelson was hardened against death, he was far from indifferent to the difficulties of life for those around him.

❧

"Here I am, one day precisely like the other . . . and some ball may soon close all my accounts with this world of care and vexation!"
Written from HMS *Victory* off Toulon to Lady Hamilton,
October 1803

Once again, Nelson returns to the theme of a cannon ball that is destined to end his life. There is reason to believe that he increasingly sensed that his death was near, only it was to arrive at Cape Trafalgar in the form of a musket ball from a sniper's weapon rather than the larger variety from a cannon.

❧

"[S]ome of us are always called before the others, and we know not whose turn may be next. We none of us can escape the grim gentleman."
Written from HMS *Victory* off Toulon to William Williams,
October 1803

These words were written in condolence, and the reference to some being called before others is another suggestion of Nelson's premonition of death.

❧

"I have no fears for the event."
Written from HMS *Victory* to Lady Hamilton, May 1804

As the Battle of Trafalgar was a little more than a year away, Nelson saw the defeat of the anticipated French invasion of Britain as the resolution of the war between the two countries. His expression of full confidence in the ability of British arms to defeat such an assault reflected his fearless approach to every battle he faced, and to life in general.

"At half-past ten drove from dear dear Merton, where I left all which I hold dear in this world, to go to serve my King and Country. May the Great God whom I adore enable me to fulfil the expectations of my Country; and if it is His good pleasure that I should return, my thanks will never cease being offered up to the Throne of His Mercy. If it is His good providence to cut short my days upon earth, I bow with the greatest submission, relying that He will protect those so dear to me, that I may leave behind."

Written on the road to Portsmouth for his private diary immediately after leaving Merton for HMS *Victory* and his final destiny at Cape Trafalgar, September 1805

This moving prayer captures much of Nelson's character. His primary focus is on doing his duty, and he expresses his willingness to give up his life in the process. He also describes in simple terms his reliance on the will of God to determine whether he was to live or die. In addition, the apparent sense of his impending death again is present in this prayer. Sadly, there was no protection following his death for the woman he held most dearly, Lady Hamilton. She lived beyond her means and died penniless in Calais, France, in January 1815; she was buried there in the graveyard of the Church of St. Pierre where she had worshipped.

"[M]y fate is fixed, and I am gone, beating down Channel with a foul wind."

Written from HMS *Victory* off Portland to his friend, Alexander Davison, September 1805

There is an ominous but accepting tone to this line as Nelson approaches his final triumph, and end, at Cape Trafalgar.

"[L]et the Battle be when it may, it will never have been surpassed. . . . If I fall on such a glorious occasion, it shall be my pride to take care that my friends shall not blush for me. These things are in the hands of a wise and just Providence, and His will be done! I have got some trifle, thank God, to leave to those I hold most dear, and I have taken care not to neglect it. Do not think I am low-spirited on this account, or fancy anything is to happen to me; quite the contrary—my mind is calm, and I have only to think of destroying our inveterate foe . . . we all hope for a meeting with the Enemy. Nothing can be finer than the Fleet under my command."

Written from HMS *Victory* to his friend, Alexander Davison, September 1805

As the culmination of Nelson's brilliant career approached, he returned to familiar themes in this revealing letter. He was sure that if he died in battle his actions would bring no dishonor to his friends and family, he had provided for those he loved, and he was totally committed to achieving a great victory over the forces that threatened Britain's security. After the chaos of many battles, the pain of numerous wounds, and the turmoil of his personal life, he had achieved a personal calm that sustained him before facing his final storm of deadly combat at Cape Trafalgar.

"I commit my life to Him who made me, and may his blessing light upon my endeavours for serving my Country faithfully. To Him I resign myself and the just cause which is entrusted to me to defend. Amen. Amen. Amen."

A portion of Nelson's last prayer, written in his private diary, 21 October 1805

As Nelson entered his final battle at Cape Trafalgar, his religious beliefs and conviction that he was fighting for a just cause were among his uppermost thoughts. *Commencement of the Battle of Trafalgar, October 21, 1805*; engraving by J. Fittler from a painting by Nicholas Pocock.

These words contain two of the most important elements that shaped Nelson's attitude about death, his deeply religious strain and his conviction that Britain's fight against Napoleon's France was a just war. Two centuries later, religious beliefs and the belief in a just cause remain important factors for those who face death in combat.

"God bless you, Blackwood, I shall never speak to you again."
Attributed by Captain Henry Blackwood, who fought at the
Battle of Trafalgar, 21 October 1805

His foreboding of death was strongly confirmed as Nelson said goodbye, as *Victory* approached within cannon shot of the enemy, to Henry Blackwood, captain of the frigate, HMS *Euryalus.*

"They have done for me at last, Hardy . . . my backbone is shot through."
Attributed to Nelson by Dr. William Beatty, surgeon aboard
HMS *Victory* at the Battle of Trafalgar, 21 October 1805

As soon as he was shot, Nelson knew that death was imminent. He accepted death as matter-of-factly as he approached battle. It was simply part of his profession as a naval officer.

"Oh, Victory, Victory, how you distract my poor brain! How dear is life to all men."
Attributed at the Battle of Trafalgar by M'Arthur and Clarke,
nineteenth century Nelson biographers, 21 October 1805

The concussion of *Victory*'s guns during the Battle of Trafalgar was so shocking that it caused Nelson, as he was dying deep below deck in the ship's cockpit, to cry out to the ship as if it was a living entity. His outcry about the dearness of life came from his recognition that soon he would lose his.

"To understand oneself is the classic form
of consolation."
—Santayana

13. Himself

*"I know myself to be so steady in my friendships, that I can-
not bear the least coolness or inattention in others."*
Written from HMS *Boreas* to his future wife, March 1786

This relatively long letter ranges over many subjects, including how anxious Nelson was to receive mail from his future
wife. His claim to steadiness in his friendships was borne out
in later years in a number of ways; one of the most striking was
his relationships with the naval officers who served with him.
This aspect of his ability to maintain steady friendships was
particularly true with that small group of extremely capable and
loyal officers—his Band of Brothers—that served under his
command.

"My activity of mind is too much for my puny constitution."
Written from Nevis to his uncle William Suckling, July 1786

A casual comment in a letter about a variety of topics shows that Nelson understood the dichotomy between his relatively frail health and his powerful internal drive for action. This contrast was to continue throughout his life, and both of these facets of his personality were ongoing subjects in his writing.

"[B]ut what I have said is the inward monitor of my heart upon every difficult occasion."
Written from Nevis to his uncle William Suckling, July 1786

One of the special qualities of Nelson's correspondence was the openness with which he described his feelings and thoughts. As he himself observed in this letter, what he wrote revealed the deeply personal forces that motivated him. His insight into his own personality, the willingness to reveal his inner thoughts, and the superior quality of his mind are elements that made his dispatches and letters such a rich source of first-hand information about the man and his times.

"Mr. Lightfoot came and paid me a visit. . . . This great attention made amends for his long neglect, and I forgot all anger; I can forgive sometimes, you will allow."
Written from HMS *Boreas* at English Harbour, Antigua, to his future wife, August 1786

This passage was part of a newsy, affectionate letter to his fiancée. The reference to the visit by a Mr. Lightfoot described a perceived slight by the gentleman, an affront that was erased by a personal visit and dinner invitation. Although Nelson could be thin-skinned at times, the light touch at the end of the comment shows that basically he lacked pomposity and frequently could smile at himself.

❧

"I fancy the King's Servants and the Officers of my little Squadron will not be sorry to part with me. They think I make them do their duty too strictly; and the West Indians will give a Balle Champetre upon my departure. They hate me; and they will every Officer who does his duty."
Written from HMS *Boreas* at English Harbour, Antigua, to his brother, the Reverend William Nelson, February 1787

For an individual who was so concerned with his reputation and honors, the animosity Nelson created with his strict enforcement in the West Indies of Britain's Navigation Acts had to concern him greatly. However, he was honest enough with himself to recognize that his actions, no matter how correct and important he believed them to be, had made him widely unpopular. With whatever faults Nelson had, this statement is evidence that self-delusion was not one of them.

In addition, the sharp difference between the dislike for him among the officers of "his little Squadron" in 1787 and the deep affection with which he was received when he returned to his powerful Mediterranean fleet in 1805 is thought-provoking.

❧

"My merit, if that is any, was seizing the happy moment."
Written from HMS *Agamemnon* off Bastia, Corsica, to his brother the Reverend William Nelson, March 1794

In writing about a successful army-navy operation ashore, Nelson highlighted one of his strengths as a combat leader, a quality that became an important part of his overall combat doctrine. At the battles of Cape St. Vincent, the Nile, Copenhagen, and Trafalgar, seizing the moment was a key to victory. And it also must be noted, his inability to do so at the Battle of Santa Cruz was a major cause of his defeat there.

❧

"We are still in the busy scene of war, a situation in which I own I feel pleasure, more especially as my actions have given great satisfaction to my Commander-in-Chief."

Written from HMS *Agamemnon* off Bastia, Corsica, to his uncle William Suckling, March 1794

Although Nelson had a fiercely independent attitude about his duty, he admitted to himself and others that he needed the approbation of those seniors he admired. When this letter was written, his commander in chief was Admiral Lord Hood, who had placed Nelson in command of a squadron for operations in the area of Corsica. It was the kind of independent assignment Nelson treasured, one that publicly demonstrated the confidence of his senior officer. Of matching importance, it was the kind of assignment that provided an opportunity for Nelson to distinguish himself in action.

❧

"I am very busy, yet own I am in all my glory; except with you, I would not be any where but where I am, for the world."

Written from the British camp at Calvi, Corsica, to his wife, July 1794

This very brief note captured the enthusiasm of a dedicated naval officer in the thick of a campaign. However, Nelson's claim that, above all, he would prefer to be with his wife has the feel of a pro forma declaration. By this time, Nelson had gone through five years of professional inactivity at Burnham without a naval assignment, and whether he recognized it in himself or not, his ardor for his wife had diminished greatly.

"I am here the reed amongst the oaks: all the prevailing disorders have attacked me, but I have not strength for them to fasten upon: I bow before the storm, whilst the sturdy oak is laid low."
Written from the British camp at Calvi, Corsica, to Prince William Henry, Duke of Clarence, August 1794

In this interesting observation Nelson made about himself, the analogy is only partially valid. Although Nelson did not have a powerful physique, he correctly pointed out that he survived many wounds and ailments that would have disabled more physically powerful men. On the other hand, his self comparison to a reed is somewhat off the mark in a different respect. His iron will was unbending and that unquestionably was one of the most important factors in overcoming his lack of physical power.

"In short, I wish to be an Admiral, and in the command of the English Fleet; I should very soon either do much, or be ruined. My disposition cannot bear tame and slow measures. Sure I am, had I commanded our Fleet on the 14th, that either the whole French Fleet would have graced my triumph, or I should have been in a confounded scrape."
Written from HMS *Agamemnon* at Fiorenzo to his wife, April 1795

This blunt self-appraisal was part hubris and part disappointment. Several weeks prior, the British fleet, of which Nelson and *Agamemnon* were parts, came in contact with a French fleet out of Toulon. Admiral Sir William Hotham, in command of the British force, broke off the action before a major battle was joined. Although Nelson had acquitted himself extremely well in the limited action, he was vociferously agitated over Hotham's failure to seize the opportunity for an all-out battle.

❦

"From the vigorous measures I am taking with the Genoese, I am most unpopular here . . . but half measures will never do when I command."
Written from HMS *Agamemnon* in the Gulf of Genoa to his brother, the Reverend William Nelson, July 1795

One doubts that Nelson's recognition of the animosity of Genoa's local populace towards him had any more effect on him than the ire of the British population in the West Indies that he raised with his strict enforcement of Britain's Navigation Acts. In fact, because the enmity in the West Indies was coming from his own countrymen, and that from the Genoese was coming from foreigners, there doubtless was even less inclination to pay attention to the latter. His observation that half measures would never do when he commanded was recognition of a personality trait that dominated his entire career.

❦

"Poor Agamemnon is as near wore out as her Captain: we must both soon be laid up to repair."
Written from HMS *Agamemnon* in Vado Bay on the Riviera coast to his friend, Sir Gilbert Elliot, British Viceroy of Corsica, August 1795

Nelson and his flagship had been employed in extremely strenuous service for two years. And during that time, he suffered a wound that cost him the sight of his right eye. However, despite the accurate observation that he was as "wore out" as his flagship, he provided another example of his resilience by remaining on station in the Mediterranean. Then at the Battle of Cape St. Vincent in February of 1797, he began his series of unprecedented major naval successes that dramatically culminated at Cape Trafalgar in October 1805.

"I have not (which probably you know) been on former occasions backward in representing to Admiral Hotham my thoughts."

> Written from HMS *Agamemnon* in Genoa harbor to
> Vice Admiral Sir Hyde Parker, November 1795

Nelson realized that one of his most prominent characteristics was his propensity to speak bluntly to his seniors, and one can imagine him writing these lines with the hint of a smile. For those who appreciated Nelson's abilities his willingness to speak his mind was welcome. For others, it was interpreted as impertinence.

Nearly six years later, as second in command to Hyde Parker in the Baltic, Nelson managed this side of his personality with restraint. As a result, and notwithstanding his frustration with the situation, Nelson was able to convince a reticent Hyde Parker to allow him to lead a detached squadron against the Danes at Copenhagen. The outcome was a victory that had immense strategic consequences for Britain.

"I reflect that I have had the unbounded confidence of three Commanders-in-Chief, I cannot but feel a conscious pride, and that I possess abilities."

> Written from HMS *Agamemnon* in the Gulf of Genoa
> to his wife, April 1796

Nelson's recognition of his own abilities, which were confirmed by his senior commanders, was more than a source of pride to him. That well-founded self-confidence significantly contributed to his willingness to risk his career. That willingness to put his career on the line was well established by 1796, and it was a crucial factor over the final, history-making nine years of his career.

"I assure you it has gone much against me to fish in Diplomatic water, for there must be many forms in getting through these matters which I am unacquainted with."
                    Written from HMS *Captain* to Francis Drake,
                        British Minister at Genoa, September 1796

Nelson was generally impatient in diplomatic matters and freely admitted it to himself and others. But his assignments in the Mediterranean constantly required diplomatic interaction. Those matters ranged from the securing of basic naval supplies and ship repairs to the maintenance of essential alliances.

At the time of this letter, he was experiencing extreme difficulty in his relations with Genoa, one of the small states of northern Italy that was both important and troublesome to Britain. Later in the letter, Nelson summarizes his difficulty with his sailor's blunt and accurate analysis of how the Genoese justified their behavior towards him. He described their attitude as, "[W]e had better offend the English than them (the French), for they will not injure us so much." In one important later event, the Battle of Copenhagen, Nelson's no-nonsense, sailor's approach to diplomacy was to work in his and Britain's favor.

"I expect nothing, and therefore shall not be disappointed: the pleasure of my own mind will be my reward. I am more interested, and feel a greater satisfaction, in obtaining yours and my father's applause, than that of all the world besides."
                Written from HMS *Captain* to his wife, November 1796

This statement about his own character gets very close to the essence of why it was possible for Nelson to stubbornly rely on his own judgment at crucial decision points. The first part of this passage echoes John Milton's lines from *Paradise Lost,* "The mind is its own place, and in itself Can make a Heav'n of Hell, a Hell of Heav'n." Nelson's reference to the pleasures of "his own mind" being their own reward intriguingly contrasts with his admitted craving for the praise of others.

The second part of this self-analysis, particularly the reference to his wife's applause, focuses on what was to become an overriding marital problem for him; he never received the degree of understanding and praise from her that he knew he needed.

"I always act as I feel right, without regard to custom."
Written from HMS *La Minerve* to his father, January 1797

This bit of personal insight went far beyond the situation he was describing to his father; it summed up much of Nelson's approach to life. It applied to how he defined his duty, how he defined his relationship with Lady Hamilton, and how he developed his combat tactics.

"[B]ut in war much is left to Providence."
Written from HMS *La Minerve* to his wife, January 1797

The fact that Nelson always acted, as he admitted, "as I feel right, without regard to custom," raised the question of what contributed to that feeling of rightness for a given decision. This statement was one of many in which he recognized his strong religious beliefs, and it helps to answer that question.

"My late Affair here will not, I believe, lower me in the opinion of the world. I have had flattery enough to make me vain, and success enough to make me confident."
Written from HMS *Theseus* to his wife, July 1797

This comment on his state of mind after the Battle of Cape St. Vincent shows Nelson's ability, at times, to analyze himself with uncanny accuracy. His recognition in himself of the two related personality qualities, vanity and confidence, was dead accurate. Both qualities were factors during the events leading up to the forthcoming Battle of Santa Cruz and in the battle itself. And in those few weeks before the event he was strongly influenced by the sum of vanity and confidence, overconfidence.

As a result of that overconfidence, the assault on Santa Cruz was an unequivocal military defeat, and he lost his right arm from a wound suffered during the fighting. However, the defeat tempered his vanity, and thanks in large part to the astute handling of the situation by his then–commander in chief, Admiral Sir John Jervis, his confidence eventually was restored to full measure.

"I ought not to call what has happened to the Vanguard by the cold name of accident: I believe firmly, that it was the Almighty's goodness, to check my consummate vanity. I hope it has made me a better Officer, as I feel confident it has made me a better Man."

Written from HMS *Vanguard* at St. Peter's Island,
Sardinia, to his wife, May 1798

The sea teaches hard lessons. And by Nelson's own admission, the ferocious storm that struck his small squadron on 20 May 1798 was a defining semester for him. Nelson's friend and flag captain of *Vanguard,* Edward Berry, described the feeling among the force before the storm. He wrote of "being elated beyond description at being so fortunate as to be the detached Squadron in the Mediterranean, and surrounded by Enemies." By the time the storm subsided, the squadron was dispersed and *Vanguard* was grievously damaged and virtually at the mercy of the sea.

It was an officer whom Nelson held in low esteem, Captain Alexander Ball in HMS *Alexander,* who rescued *Vanguard.* In a truly Nelsonian action, Ball refused Nelson's order to get *Alexander* out of danger and cast off his tow of *Vanguard,* and Ball and his crew managed to get both ships clear of the shore on which they were being driven. Nelson was quick and public in his praise of Ball's seamanship and his disobedience to his order to cast off the tow. Subsequently, they became fast friends, as Nelson repeatedly demonstrated his changed attitude towards Ball and his full confidence in his abilities.

Nelson's reference to the checking of his vanity implied a whole series of lessons learned about the sea and seamen. It also showed that he was capable of admitting his weaknesses to himself and others and learning from his mistakes.

"That the accidents which have happened to the Vanguard were a just punishment for my consummate vanity, I most humbly acknowledge, and kiss the rod which chastised me. I hope it has made me a better Officer, as I believe it has made me a better man. On the Sunday evening I thought myself in every respect one of the most fortunate men, to command such a Squadron in such a place, and my pride was too great for man; but I trust my friends will think that I bore my chastisement like a man; and it has pleased God to assist us with His favour, in our exertions to refit the Vanguard, and here I am again off Toulon."

Written from HMS *Vanguard* off Toulon to
Admiral Earl St. Vincent, May 1798

This confession to his commander in chief of his previous excess of pride shows that Nelson had returned to a more realistic view of his own abilities, considerable as they were. His confession also showed that, notwithstanding his unusually strong ego, he often was able to see his own shortcomings quite clearly.

⌒⌐

"If I have wrote my mind too freely, I trust it will be excused. The importance of the subject called for my opinion. I have given it like an honest man, and shall wish to stand or fall with it."

Written from HMS *Vanguard* to Sir William Hamilton, British Ambassador to the Kingdom of the Two Sicilies, June 1798

In this letter Nelson delivered a detailed argument for the Two Sicilies to provide the logistical support he needed to maintain his difficult and frustrating search for Napoleon's fleet. He realized that his letter was less diplomatic than what might be expected from a junior rear admiral writing to a senior British ambassador. Fortunately, Hamilton admired Nelson and was undoubtedly patient with Nelson's lack of diplomatic finesse. Nelson's ability to see his own actions with significant objectivity—and his accompanying candor—were factors in his makeup that worked to his advantage at times. His negotiations with the Danes after the Battle of Copenhagen were an outstanding example of that.

⌒⌐

"[If] you should go home, I shall be unfit for this command, where I want so many indulgences."

Written from HMS *Vanguard* to Admiral Earl St. Vincent, September 1798

Nelson was not well when he wrote this letter; he had received a head wound at the Battle of the Nile, probably involving a serious concussion, and was suffering from a fever. Notwithstanding those distractions, he recognized that he benefited from a special relationship with St. Vincent, who focused on Nelson's unique leadership capabilities rather than on his shortcomings.

~

"If God knows my heart, it is amongst the most humble of the creation, full of thankfulness and gratitude."
Written from Naples to Earl Spencer, First Lord of the Admiralty, September 1798

This statement about himself provided one of the many glimpses of the private person that Nelson wove through his correspondence. In this instance, his humbleness before his God provided a striking contrast with his ongoing hunger for public acclaim.

~

" I am not surprised that you wish him (Captain Thomas Troubridge) near you; but I trust you will not take him from me. I know he is my superior; and I so often want his advice and assistance."
Written from Naples to Admiral Earl St. Vincent, September 1798

This very unofficial admission to his commander in chief about Captain Troubridge, his military junior and long-standing friend, is another of Nelson's statements about himself that stands in clear contrast to his image as an extreme egotist. It also is another example from Nelson's writing that implied even more about him than the actual words revealed. In this instance it was a totally unselfconscious admission by Nelson to his superior that, although he might be the "Hero of the Nile," he needed the support of his fellow officer who was—in some ways other than rank—his superior. The fact that Nelson could admit that to himself and others was a manifestation of his inner strength.

⤳

"I own, my dear Lord, myself much fitter to be the actor, than the counsellor of proper measures to be pursued, in this very critical situation of public affairs; but, at least, their Sicilian Majesties are satisfied that my poor opinion is an honest one."
Written from Palermo to Admiral Earl St. Vincent,
April 1799

Nelson did not see himself as a traditional diplomat in negotiations with foreign governments. However he, and other British navy senior officers, frequently found themselves thrust into that role, and Nelson's awareness that he was not a professional diplomat allowed him to act unconventionally—at times, effectively—in his straightforward way.

In terms of the Kingdom of the Two Sicilies, Nelson had the special situation of his friendship with the British Ambassador, Sir William Hamilton, and his burgeoning romance with Lady Hamilton, who was a special confidante of the Queen. The latter relationship was both an advantage in the political leverage it provided and a disadvantage in the resulting perception of undue influence over Nelson that it created.

⤳

"I would risk my life, much less my commission, to serve my Country."
Written from HMS *Vanguard* near Ustica to Lady Hamilton,
May 1799

In this letter to his paramour and confidante, Nelson raised the possibility that an officer had justified inaction by sheltering himself "under *nice punctilios* of orders." And by this point in his career, he had clearly and repeatedly proclaimed his willingness to depart from orders to achieve what he saw as the large objective in a situation.

"But my character is, that I will not suffer the smallest tittle of my command to be taken from me; but with pleasure I give way to my friends, among whom I beg you will allow me to consider you."

Written from Palermo to Captain Sir Sidney Smith,
HMS *Tigre*, August 1799

Smith held the unusual position of both an active naval officer and an official British diplomat. As a naval officer, he was subordinate to Nelson as long as he was in Nelson's Mediterranean theater. As the minister plenipotentiary to the Sublime Porte of Turkey, he was senior to Nelson in diplomatic matters. This conflicting combination of overlapping Whitehall-Admiralty credentials was deeply resented by Nelson. He complained strenuously about the situation but with no effect. This straightforward observation about his own character was both a declaration to Smith that he would not give up any command authority and an accommodation with the reality created by Whitehall and the Admiralty.

"I know it is my disposition, that difficulties and dangers do but increase my desire of attempting them."

Excerpt from Nelson's *Sketch of My Life* written for John M'Arthur, author, October 1799

This flash of personal insight came at the end of a description of how Nelson, as a young lieutenant, had aggressively volunteered for the difficult boarding of a prize in heavy weather. His anecdote revealed how accurately he perceived this important trait in his personality. At times, such as the Battle of Santa Cruz, this drive to overcome difficult challenges got Nelson into situations that he labeled a "confounded scrape." At other times, such as the battles of the Nile, Copenhagen, and Trafalgar, it drove him to awe-inspiring and history-shaping combat victories.

❦

"The first act of my command was to name Sidney Smith's First Lieutenant to the death-vacancy of Captain Miller. . . . I own I am jealous of being trampled upon, but my disposition, as a Public man, is to reward merit, find it where I may."
Written from Palermo to Earl Spencer, First Lord of the Admiralty, November 1799

The special status of Sidney Smith as both naval officer and diplomatic minister rankled Nelson. But he accurately pointed out that his recognition of his duty to reward those who earned promotion, even if they were under the command of Smith, was more important. It was one of many situations where he made it clear that the good of the service was an extremely high priority in his scheme of things.

❦

"[N]ot a moment should be lost in attacking the Enemy. . . . The only consideration in my mind is, how to get at them with the least risk to our Ships. . . . The measure may be thought bold, but I am of opinion the boldest measures are the safest."
Written from HMS *St. George* to Admiral Sir Hyde Parker, March 1801

In this statement to Hyde Parker, Nelson accurately summarizes much of his approach to combat. At the time, Nelson was dealing with a commander in chief who clearly was not anxious for combat, but he won the argument over tactics with his superior. He also won the battle with the Danes at Copenhagen only a few days later.

❦

"[S]eamen are but bad negotiators—for we put the matter to issue in five minutes what Diplomatic forms would be five months doing."

Written from HMS *St. George* in the Baltic to Earl Carysfort, Envoy Extraordinary to the King of Prussia, May 1801

In early April of 1801, a British navy squadron commanded by Nelson defeated the Danes at the Battle of Copenhagen. At the point at which the victory was assured, Nelson arranged a truce that was uncharacteristic of his usual battle doctrine. Immediately after that truce, and in negotiations that followed, he showed that not only was he not a bad negotiator, but that his blunt approach could produce good results for Britain. A case can be made that Nelson really didn't believe that he was a bad negotiator, and that his modesty in this regard was an effective gambit.

"Oh! how I hate to be stared at!"

Written from Sheerness to Lady Hamilton, August 1801

The fame that Nelson so strongly craved also had its negative aspect for him. This emotional complaint showed that, as with many celebrities, he did not always find constant public attention pleasant.

"[I]f it be a sin to covet glory, I am the most offending soul alive."

Written from HMS *Amazon* to Admiral Lord St. Vincent, First Lord of the Admiralty, September 1801

Nelson's critics accurately point out that he was powerfully driven by vanity. On the other hand, he did not suffer from an inability to apply accurate self-analysis. This ability to see himself with considerable clarity was an important reason why he maintained strong loyalty among the officers and men of his ships and fleets.

≈

"I have made a very small purchase, and live retired, although we live so near London; for I hate the noise, bustle, and falsity of what is called the great world."
Written from Merton to Sir Brooke Boothby, May 1802

It is hard not to surmise that, at this point, what Nelson also was revealing was how he hated the disapproval of his relationship with Lady Hamilton among London's political and social leaders. And to make matters worse, there was the concomitant ridicule they were subjected to by segments of the press.

≈

"The sons of Brother-Officers have an undoubted claim to our protection, and when to that is added the son of a very old friend, nothing can, my dear Lord, weigh stronger with me."
Written from HMS *Victory* off Toulon to Admiral
Lord Radstock, August 1803

Tradition, nepotism, and a powerful fraternal sense were tightly interwoven strands in the fabric that was the British navy of Nelson's time. Nelson pointed out that he accepted all of this when it came to the son of a brother officer. Admiral Lord Radstock had fought alongside Nelson at the Battle of Cape St. Vincent, and Nelson was fully committed to helping his son in his naval career. The young man eventually was assigned, as an acting lieutenant, to *Victory* while she was still Nelson's flagship. He was transferred out of *Victory* before the Battle of Trafalgar, and he eventually became a flag officer.

Lord Radstock revealed how emotional the ties involved were. He wrote to Nelson, "Such commendation from such a man as yourself, is of that value, that no pen can describe. It will

Nelson's final self-evaluation was "Thank God I have done my duty." *Nelson in the* Victory's *Cockpit, Mortally Wounded, October 21, 1805;* engraving by R. Golding, from a painting by Benjamin West.

not only be an everlasting spur to himself, but the sight of your letter (for it shall never perish in the family, if I can help it) shall fill the breast of even his son's son with that noble fire, which can alone lead to glorious and immortal actions."

"I am not a money-getting man, for which I am probably laughed at."
> Written from HMS *Victory* to Captain Samuel Sutton,
> HMS *Amphion*, August 1804

There was something plaintive and a bit bitter in this piece of self evaluation. It was true that Nelson had invariably gravitated towards the missions that involved an opportunity for honor in combat, rather than prize money. As a result, he never gathered great wealth, and much of the money that he did manage to accumulate was used for the benefit of others.

"Nelson never has, nor can change."
> Written from HMS *Victory* to Earl Spencer, October 1804

Earl Spencer, as First Lord of the Admiralty in 1798, was a significant factor in Nelson being given command of the squadron that reestablished British naval presence in the Mediterranean in that year. In this letter six years later about Spencer's son, a naval officer, Nelson indicated that he would show "my regard for the Father by attention to the Son." His comment in the letter about never changing related specifically to his positive attitude about assisting the relatives of members of the British navy community. However, this point-blank self-analysis can be applied more generally; Nelson's essential character changed little during his thirty-five-year naval career.

*"I own myself one of those who do not fear the shore, for hardly
any great things are done in a small Ship by a man that is."*
Written from HMS *Victory* to Lord Melville, First Lord
of the Admiralty, March 1805

This bit of personal insight illuminates two special aspects of
Nelson's seamanship. One was his confidence when he was in or
close to shoal waters; another was his understanding that there
were times when risking a vessel in those waters was inherent in
carrying out one's mission. Because of his early experiences in
the small waters along the Norfolk coast and as a midshipman
in command of a cutter at the mouth of the Thames, he was less
intimidated by shallows than many other seamen.

These qualities were significant in two of his most important
victories, the battles of the Nile and Copenhagen. In both
instances, Nelson accepted the risks inherent in attacking an
enemy anchored in proximity to shoal waters, and this contributed to the audacity of his attacks. In both instances, ships
in his force actually went aground, but their groundings did not
materially affect the outcomes of the battles.

"I have not been a great sinner."
Attributed by Doctor Beatty, *Victory*'s surgeon at the
Battle of Trafalgar, 21 October 1805

In his dying hours, Nelson's brief observation about himself was
among those last words. It was his final, and provocative, assessment of himself.

Notes

Chapter 1. Duty

1. The Navigation Acts were a series of British laws passed in the seventeenth and eighteenth centuries to protect British trade and domestic industries against foreign competition. They were part of a mercantilist economic policy that required a favorable balance of trade.

2. Shakespeare, in the fourth act soliloquy of *King Henry V,* wrote:
   "We few, we happy few, we band of brothers;
   For he to-day that sheds his blood with me
   Shall be my brother. . . ."

Chapter 2. Toughness

1. The mutinies at Spithead in April and the Nore in May became the most celebrated of the uprisings in the British navy during 1797.

2. Besides round shot, the warships of Nelson's time fired a variety of charges that were designed to inflict damage to rigging and personnel at close range. These included langrage, bar, chain, and grape.

3. Lloyd's maintains a unique collection of Nelson memorabilia at their corporate headquarters in London. The collection can be viewed by making special arrangements with Lloyd's.

Chapter 3. Combat

1. In a letter to Lady Hamilton on 1 October 1805, only weeks before the Battle of Trafalgar, Nelson wrote about the reaction of his captains to his battle plans: "[W]hen I came to explain to them the *'Nelson touch,'* it was like an electric shock."

2. See Mahan's *The Influence of Sea Power upon History* (Mineola, N.Y.: Dover Publications, 1987) and Julian Corbett's *Some Principles of Maritime Strategy* (Annapolis, Md.: Naval Institute Press, 1988).

Chapter 5. Politics

1. This landmark building is on Whitehall in London and within sight of the Nelson Column at Trafalgar Square. It was designed by Thomas Ripley and erected between 1723 and 1725. The building's Board Room basically has been unchanged for 300 years and, until recent times, it was the focal point of British historic naval planning and decisions.

2. On 27 March 1802, the Treaty of Amiens established peace between Britain and France. The terms returned many of Britain's military conquests during the Napoleonic Wars to France and her allies. Ceylon (modern Sri Lanka) and Trinidad were exceptions. France evacuated Naples, Egypt, and the Papal States. War with France resumed in 1803.

Chapter 6. Armies

1. For many years, it was believed that Gutiérrez had a vast superiority of numbers in his battle against Nelson. More recent studies indicate that there was rough numerical parity between the attackers and defenders, and that Gutiérrez's leadership was an even more important factor in the battle than previously believed.

Chapter 8. Sea Power

1. In addition to Denmark, the nations that were allied in the League of Armed Neutrality included Russia, Sweden, and Prussia.

Chapter 10. Fanny and Emma

1. Emma Lady Hamilton was born in 1765 in the Village of Denhall, Cheshire. Her father, Henry Lyon, was the village blacksmith. She

and her mother used the name of Cadogan, claiming that Henry Lyon was really the disinherited heir of a Cheshire landowner named Cadogan. Emma worked as a nursemaid and lived for a time in a brothel, although there is no evidence that she was a prostitute. In London she was an artist's model, posing for both Romney and Hoppner, and became the mistress of several well-to-do men, including Charles Greville, Sir William Hamilton's nephew.

2. Frances Lady Nelson, lived out her life after Nelson's death in quiet dignity. She remained close to her son, Josiah, who died shortly before she did, and other members of the Nelson family. She died in London on 6 May 1831 at the age of seventy-three and was buried next to Josiah.

3. Emma Lady Hamilton died at Calais on 15 January 1815, was buried in a local cemetery, and later reinterred. The site of her final interment is not known. A monument to her was placed in Parc Richelieu in 1994 in the area of her original grave.

Bibliography

The primary public source for those interested in knowing more about Nelson's written words is the seven-volume *The Dispatches and Letters of Vice Admiral Lord Viscount Nelson,* edited by Sir Nicholas Harris Nicolas and first published by Henry Colburn, London, over the period 1844–46. Although "improved" copies of some dispatches and letters that were no longer available in original form were used as source material for Nicolas's work, his seven-volume collection has formed the bedrock for study of Nelson for many years. One of the special features of what has become known as The Nicolas is the work's extensive footnotes, in themselves a unique source of information about Nelson.

In 1997, Chatham Publishing in London republished The Nicolas in an affordable paperback edition. This facsimile version of the original seven volumes benefits from the excellent foreword by Michael Nash, one of Britain's leading experts on Nelson literature and the author of this book's foreword. Following is a list by general categories of books about Admiral Lord Nelson. It is by no means all-inclusive and will, no doubt, become dated as new books about Britain's greatest naval hero continue to emerge during Britain's dedicated Decade of Nelson, which will reach its climax on 21 October 2005. In some instances, there are later editions of some of the best-known biographies listed. Notable examples include Carola Oman's *Nelson* and Robert Southey's *The Life of Nelson.*

Books Based on Nelson's Own Writing
(Other than The Nicolas)

Nelson, Horatio. *Letters from Lord Nelson.* Compiled by Geoffrey Rawson. London and New York: Staples Press, 1949.

Nelson, Horatio. *Nelson's Letters to His Wife and Other Documents, 1785–1831.* Edited by George P. B. Naish. New York: Routledge and Kegan Paul, 1958.

Nelson, Horatio. *The Nelson Touch: An Anthology of Lord Nelson's Letters.* Compiled by Clemence Dane. London and Toronto: William Heinemann Ltd., 1942.

Pettigrew, Thomas Joseph. *Memoirs of the Life of Vice-Admiral Lord Viscount Nelson.* London: T. and W. Boon, 1849.

Biographies

Bennett, Geoffrey. *Nelson the Commander.* New York: Charles Scribner's Sons, 1972.

Beresford, Charles Lord and Wilson, H. W. *Nelson and His Times.* London: Harmsworth Brothers Ltd., 1897–1898.

Bradford, Ernle. *Nelson, the Essential Hero.* New York and London: Harcourt Brace Jovanovich, 1977.

Callender, Geoffrey. *The Life of Nelson.* London, New York, Bombay, Calcutta: Longmans, Green & Co., 1912.

Churchill, T. O. *The Life of Lord Viscount Nelson.* London: J. and W. MacGavin, 1808.

Clarke, James and M'Arthur, John. *The Life of Admiral Lord Nelson.* London: T. Cadwell and W. Davis, 1809.

Forester, C. S. *Lord Nelson.* Indianapolis: The Bobbs-Merrill Company, 1929.

Hibbert, Christopher. *Nelson, A Personal History.* London, New York, Victoria, Toronto, Auckland: Viking/The Penguin Group, 1994.

Howarth, David and Howarth, Stephen. *Nelson, the Immortal Memory.* London: J. M. Dent & Sons Ltd., 1988.

Kerr, Mark. *The Sailor's Nelson.* London: Hurst & Blackett, Ltd., 1932.

Mahan, Alfred Thayer. *The Life of Nelson.* Boston: Little, Brown, and Company, 1897.

Oman, Carola. *Nelson.* London: Hodder & Staughton Ltd., 1947.

Pocock, Tom. *Horatio Nelson.* London: The Bodley Head, 1987.

Russell, W. Clark. *Pictures from the Life of Nelson.* New York: Dodd, Mead and Company, 1897.

Southey, Robert. *The Life of Lord Nelson.* London: John Murray, 1813.

Walder, David. *Nelson.* New York: The Dial Press/James Wade, 1978.

Warner, Oliver. *A Portrait of Lord Nelson.* Hammondsworth, UK: Penguin Books Ltd., 1987.

Wilkinson, Clennell. *Nelson.* London, Bombay, Sydney: George G. Harrap & Co. Ltd., 1931.

Battles

Corbett, J. S. *The Campaign of Trafalgar.* London: Longmans, Green and Co., 1910.

Gardiner, Robert (ed.). *The Campaign of Trafalgar, 1803–1805.* London: Chatham Publishing, 1997.

Harbron, John D. *Trafalgar and the Spanish Navy.* London: Conway Maritime Press, 1988.

Howarth, David. *Trafalgar: The Nelson Touch.* New York: Atheneum, 1969.

Lavery, Brian. *Nelson and the Nile.* London: Chatham Publishing, 1998.

Lyon, David. *Sea Battles in Close-Up: The Age of Nelson.* Annapolis, Md.: Naval Institute Press, 1996.

Marcus, G. J. *The Age of Nelson: The Royal Navy in the Age of Its Greatest Power and Glory.* New York: The Viking Press, 1971.

Pope, Dudley. *Decision at Trafalgar.* Philadelphia and New York: J. B. Lippincott Company, 1960.

Pope, Dudley. *The Great Gamble: Nelson at Copenhagen.* New York: Simon and Schuster, 1972.

Schom, Alan. *Trafalgar: Countdown to Battle.* London: Michael Joseph, 1990.

Tracy, Nicholas. *Nelson's Battles: The Art of Victory in the Age of Sail.* Annapolis, Md.: Naval Institute Press, 1996.

Warner, Oliver. *The Battle of the Nile.* London: B T Batsford Ltd., 1960.

Warner, Oliver. *Nelson's Battles.* London: B T Batsford Ltd., 1965.

Warner, Oliver. *Trafalgar.* London: B T Batsford Ltd., 1961.

Books about Nelson and Particular Subjects

Callo, Joseph F. *Legacy of Leadership: Lessons from Admiral Lord Nelson.* Central Point, Oreg.: Hellgate Press, 1999.

Dawson, Warren R. *The Nelson Collection at Lloyd's.* London: Macmillan & Co., 1932.

Deane, Anthony. *Nelson's Favourite: HMS* Agamemnon *at War, 1781–1809.* Annapolis, Md.: Naval Institute Press, 1998.

Fitchett, W. H. *Nelson and His Captains.* London: Smith, Elder, & Co., 1904.

Gardiner, Robert, ed. *Fleet Battle and Blockade, The French Revolutionary War 1793–1797.* London: Chatham Publishing, 1996.

Gardiner, Robert, ed. *Nelson Against Napoleon.* Annapolis, Md.: Naval Institute Press, 1997.

Kennedy, Ludovic. *Nelson's Captains.* New York and London: W. W. Norton & Company, 1951.

King, Dean and Hattendorf, John B., eds. *Every Man Will Do His Duty: An Anthology of Firsthand Accounts from the Age of Nelson.* New York: Henry Holt and Company, 1997.

Laughton, J. K. *Nelson and His Companions in Arms.* London: Longmans, Green & Co., 1896.

Lavery, Brian. *Nelson's Navy.* Annapolis, Md.: Naval Institute Press, 1989.

Mackenzie, Robert Holden. *The Trafalgar Roll.* Annapolis, Md.: Naval Institute Press, 1989.

Masefield, John. *Sea Life in Nelson's Time.* London: Conway Maritime Press, 1984.

McKay, John. *The 100-Gun Ship* Victory. London: Conway Maritime Press Ltd., 1987.

Morriss, Roger. *Nelson: The Life and Letters of a Hero.* London: Collins & Brown Ltd., 1996.

Moorhouse, E. Hallam. *Nelson in England: A Domestic Chronicle.* London: Chapman & Hall Ltd., 1913.

O'Brian, Patrick. *Men-of-War: Life in Nelson's Navy.* New York and London: W. W. Norton & Company, 1995.

Orde, Denis A. *Nelson's Mediterranean Command: Concerning Pride, Preferment and Prize Money.* Edinburgh, Cambridge, Durham, UK: The Pentland Press Ltd., 1977.

Pocock, Tom. *Nelson's Women.* London: André Deutsch Limited, 1999.

Pope, Dudley. *Life in Nelson's Navy.* Annapolis, Md.: Naval Institute Press, 1981.

Remembering Nelson: A Record of the Lily Lambert McCarthy Collection at the Royal Naval Museum, Portsmouth, as told to Lieutenant Commander John Lea, RN. Published privately in association with the Royal Naval Museum, 1995.

Russell, Jack. *Nelson and the Hamiltons.* New York: Simon and Schuster, 1972.

Warner, Oliver, ed. *Nelson's Last Diary.* Kent, Ohio: The Kent State University Press, 1971.

White, Colin. *1797: Nelson's Year of Destiny.* Gloucestershire, UK: Sutton Publishing Ltd. in association with the Royal Naval Museum, 1998.

White, Colin, ed. *The Nelson Companion.* Annapolis, Md.: Naval Institute Press, 1995.

Index

ABOUT THE AUTHOR

Joseph F. Callo, a retired rear admiral in the U.S. Naval Reserve, was commissioned from the Yale University Naval Reserve Officers Training Corps in 1952 and assigned to sea duty with the Atlantic Amphibious Force. Two years later he went back to civilian life, briefly returning to active duty for a special assignment in the pre-commission detail of USS *Saratoga*. As a civilian Callo held senior positions with major advertising agencies and was a television producer for PBS and NBC, where he earned a Peabody Broadcasting Award. He also earned creative awards as a TV scriptwriter. He taught advertising and writing for the mass media as an adjunct professor at St. John's University in New York City. Now a freelance writer on military, travel, and corporate subjects, Callo was named author of the year by *Naval History* magazine in 1998. His book *Legacy of Leadership: Lessons from Admiral Lord Nelson,* was published in 1999 and his articles regularly appear in leading magazines and newspapers throughout the country. He divides his time between New York City and Kansas City, Missouri.